HOW DOES THE STOCK MARKET WORK

A Beginner's Guide to Highly Profitable Stocks

Table of Contents

Introduction

The key to creating wealth from investing is knowing how to make positive returns from the majority of your investments. This can only be achieved by an investor with a thirst for knowledge on how to implement most theoretical investment concepts. This book was written to aid all those with that desire to learn and it offers practical insights on how to apply stock investment strategies and make positive returns from investing.

Chapter 1 introduces the stock market and explains in detail how an individual can invest in the stock market. The chapter also details the potential gains of investing in the stock market and the advantages that accrue to those who do. With investments come risks. It should be understood from the onset that investing in stock is risky. Just as much as there is a potential to make profits, the possibility that one may lose a significant amount of their hard-saved money is very real.

Chapter 2 addresses common mistakes that result in stock investors losing money and also guides investors on how to be skillful in stock market investments. One of the reasons why this book was written was to conscientize the investor who's behind all the activity that prevails across all stock exchanges around the world—people. Ordinary people who may or may not understand how to make money and some who may be investing in the exchange for the wrong reasons altogether.

Chapter 3 unveils these faceless investors and focuses on the psychological traits and pitfalls of investors, so you can understand what it takes to make it as an investor.

The different financial assets that can be invested in in the stock market, including stock market indexes, are explained in Chapters 4 and 5.

The last three chapters focus on how to grow wealth. Chapter 6 details investment strategies for beginners, while Chapter 7 showcases the investment strategies and successes and failures of some of the richest men in the world. This is all wrapped up in the last chapter, which details the importance of financial freedom and how one can work towards creating wealth.

I would encourage those who have never invested in the stock market before to read the chapters in chronological order, as the book introduces certain concepts in the early chapters and builds upon them in later chapters. For those who are already toe-deep, or even knee-deep, in the investing game can read the book too, as each chapter is a standalone.

Chapter 1: Stock Market?

What Is the Stock Market?

Have you ever imagined yourself as a co-owner of a company like Apple? Microsoft? Facebook? Coca-Cola? These are some of the most profitable and popular companies in the world. If you could get a slice of those profits, that would be quite an amazing thing, wouldn't it? The good news is that it's possible through investing in the stock market.

Stocks, also known as shares, represent fractional ownership in a public company. What this means is that there are some companies that allow the general public to invest in them, and one does this by buying a fraction of the company in the form of shares. As part-owner of a company, a shareholder is then entitled to a share in the profits of said company in the form of dividends. The shareholder will also benefit if the company becomes more valuable as seen through an increase in the price of the company's shares.

In order to be public, a company should enlist in what is known as a stock exchange, which is a regulated platform that matches buyers and sellers of shares. Most countries have a stock exchange, some with more than one.

Below are a few examples from around the world, in no particular order:

Country	Abbreviation
South Africa	JSE

Botswana	BSE
Rwanda	RSE
Zimbabwe	ZSE
United States	NYSE
United States	NASDAQ
Canada	CSE
Mexico	BMV

China	SSE
Japan	TSE
Germany	XFRA

Each of these stock exchanges is regulated by a Securities and Exchange Commission, whose role it is to protect investors by promoting fair and transparent practices by all parties active on the exchange.

Not all companies qualify to be listed on an exchange. There are listing requirements that a company has to meet to be registered. A company applies to be listed on a stock exchange, and this application can be declined if the company fails to meet all the requirements.

The first step to becoming listed is to prepare a prospectus, which is a detailed document that the company should offer to anyone interested in buying the company's shares. This prospectus describes the businesses operations, financial health, management and risk factors (Sherman, 2019).

As part of the application process, there are many documents that a company would need to submit to ensure that the investing public has complete information, which includes a copy of the corporate charter and bylaws. The applying company would need to prove that it is able to meet the stock exchange listing standards and also show that the business is in good standing in the state/country it is registered in. Being listed is a mark of prestige

(Sherman, 2019).

All these steps ensure that only the best companies are listed on the exchanges. As an individual investor, this lessens perceived risks as these companies are bound by the stock exchange rules and regulations.

Due to globalization, markets all around the world are now accessible. With a bit of determination and research, it is possible to invest in a foreign company listed on an exchange outside your country. So, one can even invest in lucrative companies from anywhere in the world. Oh, imagine the possibilities this opens up!

The Johannesburg Stock Exchange does not trade South African stock only but has listings from other African countries such as Egypt, Kenya, Mauritius, Nigeria, Morocco, Nigeria and Tunisia, and has plans to trade shares from Ghana, Zimbabwe, Namibia and Zambia (Bluechiplist, n.d.).

As an individual, one cannot trade directly on a stock exchange. Only securities dealing with firms, commonly known as stockbroking firms, are allowed to deal in securities on a stock exchange. For example, the Zimbabwe Stock Exchange specifically states that these stockbroking firms have to demonstrate, to the satisfaction of the exchange, that they meet the following standards:

They have financial resources to meet its obligations.
They have adequate personnel, premises, communication and data processing capabilities, and records to enable it to fulfil the exchange's obligations and operational requirements.
They submit all documents and information that the exchange may, from time to time, prescribe for the use of the automated trading system.

Even with all of these standards met, stockbroking firm employees still cannot place orders or execute trades unless they are registered with the exchange as an operator. To be registered, the concerned individuals have to first undergo training on how the trading system works and demonstrate that they have the requisite knowledge and experience of market operations. The exchange also reserves the right to restrict the different types of securities that a participant may have access to for the purpose of trading.

The exchange maintains a register of all such operators. For example, the Zimbabwe Stock Exchange lists the following as some of the registered stockbrokers: Banc ABC, Akibos Securities, and Bethel Equities. Addresses and other contact information is also found on the website, making it very easy for investors to identify a broker they may want to be associated with.

It is not possible for an individual to invest directly in the stock exchange. As an individual, once you have made up your mind to invest in the stock exchange, the next stage is to look for a registered broker. A stockbroker is a professional who has been trained and registered with a particular stock exchange to buy and sell stocks on behalf of clients. These stockbrokers are also regulated by the stock exchange to ensure that investors are protected. One should thus only deal with brokers that are registered with a stock exchange and these are known as member firms. Member firms can be viewed on the stock exchange website.

When choosing a broker, you can compare them by looking at the following information:

The monthly administration fee charged.
The transactional costs that are charged for every transaction executed by a broker.
The minimum amount that should be in your trading account before you can start trading.
The ease with which you can interact with the broker, should you need support or assistance.
Information that you are likely to have access to as a client, such as the brokers daily's records, free training courses, educational material, personalized services, robot advisers, and so on.

An important distinction between brokerage firms, that can have an impact on the service fees that are charged and accessibility to foreign markets, is the availability of online services. Some brokerage firms are known as full- service brokers, and these are traditional brokers who typically offer other financial services to help with investment needs, such as tax advice and retirement planning. The other type of brokerage firm is online brokers. These brokers just provide a platform for individual investors to execute their trades. Their service is not personalized, and they do not offer any advice at all, which results in much lower transaction costs.

The Potential Gain of Investing in the Stock Market

As was explained above, shares or stocks represent fractional ownership in a company. As an investor, the ultimate goal is to make money, that is, to get a positive return on your investments. The potential gains of investing in the stock market come from two sources: dividends and capital growth.

Cash Inflows at Periodic Intervals

A dividend is a payment made by a company to its shareholders as a way to distribute its profits. Unprofitable companies cannot declare dividends. Therefore, one must do adequate research before choosing shares to buy.

Dividends provide periodic income if the company invested in pays out such dividends. Most well-established companies that have shown steady profitability over a long period of time offer regular dividend income (Amadeo, 2019). For example, on the Johannesburg Stock Exchange, some of the companies that are ranked as giving the highest and most consistent, uninterrupted dividend growth are Clientele ltd, Mondi PLC Pre, Nedbank Group, AVI

Ltd., and Nu-World Holdings (Van Vuuren, 2019), while on the New York Stock exchange there is AT&T, Chevron, Invesco, and Home Depot, amongst others (Jadeja, 2019).

Such companies, which have a long record of increasing dividends, are unlikely to skip paying dividends or to decrease dividends. These dividends are declared on a per share basis. For instance, if a company that you have bought 1,000 shares in declares a dividend of 20¢ per share, the total dividend income you would expect when the company pays out is $0.2*1,000=$200, and this will be paid out to you in cash. The expectation from investing in a dividend stock is cash inflows at periodic intervals.

Potential for High Capital Gains

There are also companies that do not consistently pay dividends. Rather, they reinvest profits back into the business. These are typically new, fast- growing, and high-risk companies with innovative business ideas that are known as growth stocks.

Such companies also offer a return, though not as periodically as dividend stocks. This return is what is called capital gains. What this means is that, as an investor, should you choose to invest in such a company, your return is likely to come from the increase in the share price. As the company reinvests its profits, you should expect that its assets base grows and its ability to make more profits in the future also grows.

This expectation of higher future profits is likely to make other investors see it as more valuable since it has more potential, which will push up its price on the stock market. It should, however, be noted that these returns cannot be realized without selling off the shares you have.

Therefore, if you invest in a non-dividend paying stock, returns can only be realized by selling off shares to take advantage of the increase in the stock price on the stock exchange. Examples of such growth stocks on the NYSE are Amazon, Carvana, and the TriNetGroup, and on the Tokyo Stock

Exchange are Sosei Group Corp. and AnGes, Inc. (Lee, 2019).

Potential for Getting a High Return on Your Investments

If you already have a savings account, should you just leave your savings in your account and hope that you will be able to raise all the money you need to do all the big things that you have always wanted? Buy that dream house? Save for retirement?

The truth is, if you are not already rich (inheritance from your parents maybe?), for most, there is a chance that you may never be able to save enough to afford everything you need. The stock market gives you an opportunity to get more returns than you could ever get by simply leaving your savings in an account that offers a measly 0.05% return.

That said, the stock market is not a get rich quick kind of investment, but the high potential returns are likely to accumulate in the long run.

Why Invest in the Stock Market

Having detailed the potential gains of investing in stocks, it is fairly obvious that most investors look for opportunities to grow their wealth in the stock market. Dividends and capital gains are a source of return that, if reinvested, can result in an investor growing their wealth with time.

Those who have good investment strategies can gain huge returns from just buying stocks at a low price and holding on to those shares until they have gone up significantly. However, investing also exposes an investor to risk.

There is a chance that some investments may lose value if the stock price goes down. Even though individual stocks on the stock exchange may present as very risky investments, the stock market provides many investors who are risk averse with a chance to invest, whilst minimizing risk. This is called diversifying.

A typical stock exchange has a number of listed shares and one can structure a portfolio using the stocks to create an investment that simply treks the overall market and has minimum risk. If you already have other investments, like bonds, adding stocks to the portfolio will minimize the overall risk as stock prices move independently.

Lastly, investing in the stock market implies that, as part-owner, you get to influence what happens in the business that you have invested in by voting on certain business decisions.

Chapter 2:
Why Do People Lose Their Money?

When one invests in stocks, the expectation is that they will make a profit. But more often than not, this does not happen. Stock prices move up and down in reaction to a number of factors, and if an investor buys at a very high price, they may not be able to make any returns if the stock price goes down.

So, what can drive a share price up or down? Understanding this is the key to successful investing. It should be understood from the onset that investing in stock is risky. Just as much as there is a potential to make profits, it is also possible to lose money. Ergo, it is very important to manage risk.

In this section, attention is paid to the most common mistakes that may result in negative returns for an investor. A negative return occurs when an investment is worth less than what was invested at the end of the investment period.

Common Mistakes in Stock Market Investment

Investing in Shares That Are Held by a Lot of Institutional Investors

A common mistake is to buy into a share that already has a lot of institutional investors. Institutional investors are entities that pool money from different sources and invest in large volumes. Examples are insurance companies and pension funds. These institutions typically have money flowing in from clients and are typically always on the lookout for investments that can earn a minimum stipulated return.

Imagine this kind of institution sets its eye on a stock that seems to offer a steady return and they decide to include such stock in its portfolio. How many shares do you think the institution will buy? 500? 1000? 10,000? I'm sure you got that right. Institutions typically buy stocks in large volumes, and though this may be spread out over days or weeks until the desired volume is reached, the sustained demand for the stock is likely to push the stock price.

However, the reverse is also true. Should the investor

then decide to remove such stock from its portfolio, what do you think would be the result on the share price? A decrease, of course. If large volumes of shares are being offloaded on the market, this is likely to result in a dip in the share price in that period. This decline in the share price is purely due to the forces of supply and demand having an effect on the share price, and this does not necessarily mean that the company itself is not doing well and one should exit the market because of the decline in the price. Therefore, investors should avoid such stocks, as they are likely to go down should the big investors start offloading them.

But how can one be able to tell if price movement in shares is due to the actions of institutional investors? The key is to look at price sheets, which should show the volumes of the stocks traded and indicate block trades. A block trade occurs when a large number of shares, usually more than 10,000, are either bought or sold at once.

An academic study conducted by Ke and Petroni (2004) showed that most institutional investors usually sell-off stock one quarter in advance, before bad news that can negatively affect stock prices is released. These findings suggest that institutional investors may have access to information that is not available to the public. They also present evidence that most companies schedule invite-only conference calls with their institutional investors before bad news is announced to the public, in order to maintain a long-term relationship of trust with institutional investors' analysts.

When the institutional investors act on this information, they are able to avoid large losses. Companies with a significant shareholding by institutions appreciate that their shares are valuable and more liquid, and therefore have an incentive to pre-empt negative news to try and maintain good relationships. If a company has a significant shareholding by institutional investors that means that the company is also likely to be better managed and likely to have a higher earning potential as investors. This is because the major shareholders are likely to monitor the actions of managers closely, resulting in a more efficient allocation of resources.

Assuming that there is nothing wrong with the fundamentals of the company, if the share price dropped due to an institutional investor selling, the price should go back up later and there is no reason to panic. However, if other investors see that institutional investors have their eye on certain stock, they usually jump onto the bandwagon too and also start buying the stock in anticipation of a price rise. The actions of institutional investors thus can be interpreted to imply something about a company's projected financial health.

This makes sense because institutional investors are typically big companies with the resources to hire the finest researchers and analysts to study the market and come up with the best buys compared to research that can be done by a novice investor. It is worth noting though that institutional investors' actions on the stock market are more often than not driven by other factors that may not be in tandem with your own needs as an individual investor. So, you should not necessarily buy or sell stocks whenever institutional investors do so.

For example, institutional investors are likely to react to news that will have a long-term impact on the share price since their investment horizons are typically longer (Ke & Petroni, 2004). As an individual, if you just blindly follow their strategies, you may miss out on opportunities to make short- term abnormal returns which you can get from reacting to news that may affect the share price in the short-term. It is worthwhile, though, to consider what is happening on the market, and to do further research on such companies to determine whether what stock suits your own investment needs.

Not Paying Attention to Your Portfolio

Prices of shares on the stock market move up, which is good. However, they also move down, which is what may result in negative returns. This movement in the share price is mainly due to investors reacting to news. If there is positive news about a company, investors react by buying more shares. The increase in demand for shares is what pushes up the price on the market. Negative news has the opposite impact.

For instance, if a company releases its financials and its reported earnings seem to be going down and that appears to be the expected trend in the   future, it is then a reasonable expectation that the stock price of such a company should then go down. If the price does not go down, it would imply that the stock is overvalued, as investors are likely to be paying more than what the share is worth. After all, as an investor (part-owner) your actual claim in the company is on the earnings, which may or may not be paid out   to you as dividends.

If earnings are going down, investors should not still be paying the same price for the stock. What then happens is that some investors, who actually pay attention to such fundamental information, may exit the market before the price falls in order to lock in capital gains. Capital gains occur when the selling price of the stock, at the end of an investment, is more than the price that was paid at the beginning of the investment.

As more and more investors dispose of their stock holding when they realize that the company is not projected to do well, this action, that is more sellers than buyers, is likely to push the price of the stock down. Again, we are seeing the forces of supply and demand at play in influencing the price of shares. So, as an investor, if you don't pay attention to your portfolio, you will miss opportunities to make super high returns by failing to act on signs that you may need to exit a certain position. By the time you want to cash in on your investment, the share prices may have fallen so low that you incur a loss.

Failing to Acknowledge Their Investment Goals

The first thing, before making the decision to put money down, is to decide what kind of return one wants from the investment, and this is partly informed by financial needs. Consider the following investors:

1.   A young couple who are both employed and have no kids.
2.   A couple that is struggling to pay off their mortgage and car loans with two children who are both going to college.
3.   A retired couple whose pension is not able to cover their annual needs.

The financial circumstances for each of these couples is very different, and this should be a major determinant of what kind of investments they are likely to make. These financial circumstances affect the expected returns, the investment horizon, and the risk appetite of the investor. Once you have determined your financial needs, these can then be crafted into investment goals. Questions that you should ask yourself before jumping into investing in the stock market are:

How much capital do you have or are willing to put towards the stock market?
What is your investment horizon? As in, how long do you want to commit the funds?
What is your risk appetite? This is determined largely in part by why you are investing in the first place. For example, investing to raise money for a child's college fund means you are likely to be risk averse as you don't want to chance losing all your investment.

The stock market, in general, is susceptible to shocks in the economy and generally does well when the economy is doing well, and vice versa. So, if an investor is not well-read about the different kinds of investment strategies that suit their investment goals and how to manage the risk that comes from investing in the stock exchange, they may be vulnerable. Questions that an investor should ask themselves before investing is: In order to meet your financial needs, do you need an investment that gives you regular income? Or do you simply want an increase in investment value, even though you might not have any regular income now. For example, if one invests in a growth stock, and there is a crisis that requires they liquidate their investment as they do not have other savings, they may then be forced to sell their shares at a price lower than what they would have bought at (sigh).

Failing to Time Their Entry and Exit in the Market

When one makes the decision that they want to invest, they do their research, and finally settle on a stock that they want to buy, it follows that the next logical thing is to take action, that is, buy the stock, right? Wrong! Stock prices move up and down depending on the level of activity on the market. If there are a lot of people in a particular trading session who want to buy the stock compared to investors who want to sell, the price of the stock is likely to be high, and if there are a lot of sellers compared to buyers, the price of the stock is likely to be low. So, once a decision has been made, the next thing to do is to watch the market and wait for the price of the stock to pull back into a price range that you are comfortable with before investing.

The price action of shares follows a zigzag pattern. The price may go up and it may go down. However, what should concern an investor is the trend line. Paying attention to the ups and downs on a daily basis means that you are likely to be caught up in all the noise and may end up deciding to exit too quickly. A trend line shows the prevailing direction of price and should be used to make entry and exit decisions.

How to Be Skillful in Stock Market Investment

Avoid Putting All Your Eggs in One Basket

Imagine you have $10,000 and you decide to invest in the stock market. It's your first time but you try to give this your best shot by researching and following the news, and you pick just one stock to invest in. If, for one reason or another, the stock price drops significantly, a huge portion of your investment will be wiped out. After all, investing in the stock market does not give you guaranteed returns. After coming up with your investment goals, in order to avoid scenarios where you are overexposed to one counter, an investor should use a concept known as diversification to reduce exposure to one stock.

Instead of investing all savings in just one stock, you can choose a number of stocks to invest in and these different counters make up what is known as a portfolio. The overall return on the portfolio may have different risk and return profiles compared to each of the individual shares when analyzed in separation. One can diversify within the stock market, as in look for other stocks to buy or alternatively diversify outside the stock market by considering other alternative investment options, such as bonds.

Know the Different Categories of Stocks

Once you have determined your investment goals, the next step is to understand the different categories that stocks can be classified into and then try to match those that you think match your investment goals. There are four categories of stock, and these are discussed below:

Dividend stocks or income stocks

These stocks offer investors a steady stream of dividends. The norm is that companies with such stocks are big companies with strong financials that no longer have room for growth. As such, instead of retaining profits for reinvestment purposes, dividends are paid to companies.

Investors holding these stocks get passive income. What this means is even   if you don't actively manage your portfolio, you are guaranteed a steady stream of income in the form of dividends. To identify such companies, an investor should look for companies with a consistent dividend paying streak, with the dividends declared increasing consistently. Given such a record, it is reasonable to assume that such a company will continue with its dividend policy in the near future.

You can also compare the dividend payout ratio of the company with that of other companies in the same industry. The payout ratio is the percentage of earnings that are paid out as dividends. A very low payout ratio means the company is retaining most of its earnings, a payout of close to 100% means the company is distributing most of its earnings as dividends, and a pay-out that is greater than 100% means the company is dipping into its reserves and paying out dividends to its shareholders that are more than its earnings. This isn't sustainable in the long run and should signal to the investor that dividends are likely to go down in the long run. In addition to the dividend payout record, which is based on past information, it is also important to   look at the business profile and outlook of the business in order to evaluate if the company is of sound business health.

Dividend stocks are suitable for investors who are looking for a reliable source of extra income. An example of such an investor is someone who is in retirement and looking to supplement their income. Suggested industries where one can find such high dividend stocks are telecommunications companies, energy providers, health stock, and real estate investment trusts.

Most brokers offer tools that can help investors screen stocks in their bid for the best dividend stocks. At the click of a button, it is possible to filter stocks using such tools as Charles Schwab's screener and SafetyNet Pro which allows the user to input a variety of selection criteria (Rains, n.d.). Examples of such criteria include regular dividend amount, payout ratio, three-, five- and ten-year dividend growth rates, and so forth. In addition to these, the user can add more criteria, such as company size and financial performance

Penny stocks

These are shares that trade at no more than $5 each. These are typically shares of small start-up companies that are looking to raise capital. These shares are very cheap. They are not listed on major stock exchanges but are traded through pink sheets and OTC Bulletin Board (OTCBB).

Penny stocks are associated with high risk, but also high reward! Trading these stocks is all about getting quick returns, and therefore they are not suited to a passive investor. To make a profit, one has to actively trade stocks and always be on the lookout for opportunities to make quick gains. The best way to do this is to register with an online broker, which would give you the platform to make your own trades.

That said, in order to successfully trade penny stocks, you would have to immerse yourself in the practical aspects that come with learning how to trade. This means studying charts, finding patterns, and forecasting. Stocks can be bought and sold within minutes and this is called day-trading.
Therefore, this kind of trading is only suitable for active traders. Given the small returns, using only cheap brokers will result in positive overall returns after costs.

Growth stocks

These companies reinvest most of their earnings and are thus characterized by zero to low dividend pay-outs. Due to reinvesting its earnings, as the company's asset base grows, revenues and earnings are expected to increase at a faster rate than average companies within the same industry.

This expectation of higher revenues in the future is expected to drive up the value of the shares on the stock exchange. Investors buy these shares in anticipation of capital gains, and some indicators that can help you identify such stocks are:

Patents or access to technologies that other industry players do not have.
A very large market share, especially if the company is reaping benefits from coming up with a very innovative idea.
Strong growth rate for the past five years, typically between 5% and 10%.

High return on equity when compared to other companies in the industry and high earning per share. A projected stock price that's expected to double.

Examples of industries with typical growth stocks are pharmaceuticals and technology companies. These types of shares are typically suitable for young investors who are willing to take on riskier investments.

Value stocks

These are undervalued stocks on the market, and investors lookout for such stocks in the hope of locking in capital gains when the market corrects itself. It is, however, important to make sure that the company is a financially sound company, as seen through current assets that are twice current liabilities, debt that is less than equity, and a low-price earnings ratio.

Possible reasons why a company may be undervalued on the stock market could be poorly a performing industry in general which causes most investor to shun such stocks, a new and unproven company that has good financials but is not yet on the radar of most institutional investors, or negative media attention resulting in a low price.

Blue-chip stocks

These are shares of large, financially sound companies with a large market capitalization that usually pay attractive dividends. In India, a few examples are Tata Consultancy Services and Reliance Industry, in the USA there is Apple and Johnson and Jonson, and in the UK, you have Royal Dutch Shell and BP.

Know What Kind of Investor You Are

Are you a short-term or long-term investor? This also has an impact on the kind of information you look for and base your decisions on. For example, long-term investors may focus on technical factors and are not necessarily influenced by short-term price fluctuations to change their stock holdings. Short-term investors, on the other hand, may focus on fundamentals and on identifying particular dips and peaks in the stock price to identify entry and exit opportunities that could maximize returns.

Liquidity

This is the ease with which an investor can enter or exit an investment position. Imagine you buy a stock, monitor its performance, and determine the best time to sell in line with your investment objectives. When the time comes for you to sell, there is no one in the market willing to buy at that price. So, what should you do if you really want to exit the position? You have to lower the price that you are willing to accept for the shares until you get someone who is willing to take up the shares.

Remember, investors are always on the lookout for undervalued shares, and if the price is much lower than the actual price of the stock, you will eventually get a taker. As such, illiquid shares, i.e. infrequently traded shares, always sell at a lower price due to this liquidity discount. Larger companies are well traded which makes them more liquid than small stocks and thus more attractive to investors. This attractiveness comes from the ease with which one can enter or exit a position without losing any value.

News

In general, news also has an impact on stock prices. There is a lot of news that can drive stock prices by impacting demand or supply of shares. For instance, xenophobia has been an issue in South Africa, and it has been widely publicized and condemned over the years. Spates of xenophobic attacks were witnessed in 2008, 2015, 2018, and 2019. This is social unrest which is external to the companies that are listed on the stock exchange, but it cannot be denied that this social arrest resulted in loss of human life, destruction of property, as shops were looted and burnt, and there is a general disruption in normal business operations.

Using data from the JSE for 2008 and 2015, during and after the xenophobic violence of these years, Ngwakwe and Ilorah (2017) showed that both the news and the actual attacks may have provoked a shock to the stock market, with the mean returns on stocks during the xenophobic attacks being less than the mean performance for the months following the xenophobic violence.

So, what does this mean for a potential investor? If you already have shareholding in a market, you should pay attention to the news, as it gives you an indication of what is likely to affect stock prices. Sources of news and how the news is likely to affect share prices are ample, instances include: reading newspapers, listening to the news on the TV or radio, and following business and finance TV shows. Zipin (2019) mentions finance documentaries and TV shows as a great source of information. Examples of such TV shows, listed in alphabetical order, are summarized below:

TV Show	Network
Charlie Rose	PBS and Bloomberg LP.
Mad Money with Jim Cramer	CNBC

Shark Tank	ABC
Squawk Box	CNBC

The Dave Ramsey Show	YouTube
The Financial Diet	YouTube
The Suze Orman Show	CNBC and YouTube
Your Money	CNN
The Profit	CNBC

Business Cycle

Predictions about the economy also affect stock

market prices in general. Economic activity is measured by GDP, which is a monetary measure of the goods and services produced by a country annually. Sometimes the recorded level of GDP is low and sometimes it is high. These swings in GDP move in a cyclical pattern, and this is referred to as the business cycle, as these swings reflect changes in economic fluctuations. A graphical representation of a business cycle is shown below:

The Economic Cycle

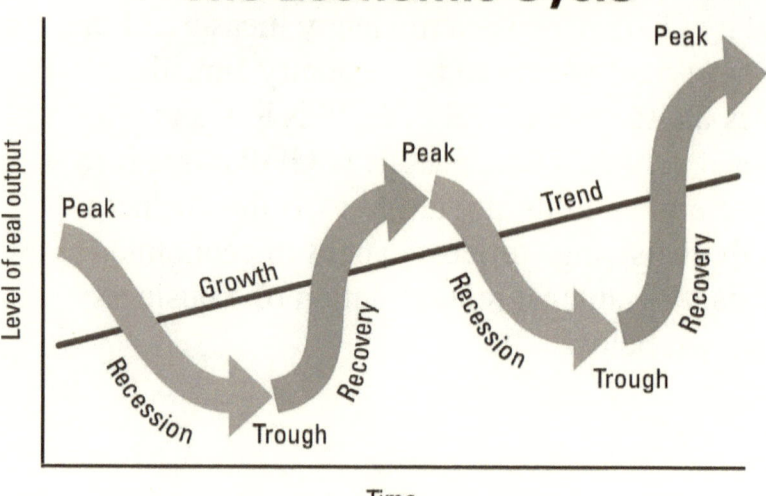

(mrshearingeconomics, n.d.)

From the diagram, four distinct phases of the economic cycle can be seen: peak, recession, trough, and recovery. In each phase, the stock market performs differently. Each phase typically lasts for years. In fact, it could last for so long that it may seem that the situation can go on indefinitely.

For example, if the economy is expected to expand as seen through an increase in gross domestic product (GDP) and decrease in unemployment level, amongst other things, consumer confidence in the economy is generally high. Companies expand as they take advantage of increases in demand for products and services, resulting in need for more fixed assets. The norm is that, during this expansion phase, most companies record significant increases in profits and are thus able to access debt finance easily to fund increases in operations. Employees also fall on good times during this period. An increase in business activity means lots of overtime work, an increase in salaries as higher profitability means the company can also afford salary increments, sizeable bonuses at the end of each year, and attractive profit-sharing schemes as management tries to keep their employees motivated to retain their skilled workers.

This description paints a very vivid picture: Highly profitable businesses with alluring financials on one hand, and on the other, a lot of employees who are experiencing a surge in income, so much so that they have budget surpluses. In such an environment, savings go up and there is a marked interest and increase in stock market activity as more and more people try to invest their surpluses for one reason or another. An increase in investor demand for stocks means low availability of stocks for sale, because who wants to dispose of shares when business is doing so well and there is an anticipation that this growth will last for years? This drives up the share price.

Do you think that the economic activity described above can go on indefinitely? Well, it doesn't. The growth described will continue, but only up to a point when the economy fails to sustain the economic activity that's happening.

Imagine a situation when demand for goods and services increases at such a pace that is unrealistic and unmatched by company growth. Full employment is reached, i.e. all those people who are economically active and want to work are employed and even working overtime, and still business is not able to satisfy all the goods and services that are demanded. What happens then? Companies may start to make reckless financing decision, such as using too much debt to try and expand in order to better serve their clients.

Banks also relax their lending criteria in such a situation as they jostle for clients. The thinking behind is that high profits imply that companies can service high debt levels. Remember, the increase in savings by individuals means that banks also have a lot of money that is available for lending.

Households that are not saving also spend recklessly and borrow more to finance purely consumptive expenditure. After all, debt is cheap. It thus makes sense to just borrow and enjoy today rather than try to save for years to go on that cruise that you have always wanted to take or to take up expensive hobbies like art collection and skydiving.

Despite all these efforts to try and meet demand on the market, the economy can get overheated. Juneja (n.d.) highlights that if actual GDP is higher than potential GDP, then this means that "humans, as well as natural resources of a country, are being utilized more than they actually should be" and that shows that the economy is overheated.

Common features of an overheated market that a stock market investor can easily spot and should look out for are:

Artificially low interest rates to encourage more borrowing as banks have a lot of money to loan out. Overpriced houses and rentals.
An increase in household indebtedness. High inflation levels. •

In such an overheated economy, share prices can actually go up to such a level that companies are overvalued on the market. When shares are overvalued, this means investors are paying much more for shares than is justifiable, given the companies' asset base and profit projections. As more and more money is available for investment, demand for shares keeps growing, and soon only the forces of supply and demand are interacting to determine price, so much so that company fundamentals, such as profitability and earnings potential, are no longer keeping up.

Some investors actually invest just to get profits from the ever-increasing prices of counters. These types of investors are called speculators—investors who are just betting on the movement of prices on the market and want to profit from that. These investors typically have short-horizon periods and will just buy shares in the hope that the share price will keep going up and they will dispose of these at a profit.

Why should an investor in the stock market care about whether the economy is overheating or not? If you are already a shareholder, identifying the symptoms of an overheating economy allows you to dispose of shares before share prices start to tumble, thus giving you a chance to reap abnormally high returns on your investment.

If you are thinking about investing in the stock market, and you can tell that the economy is overheating, would it be a good idea to go ahead and invest your money? No! Improper timing is one of the things that can lead to an investor making losses. From the diagram above on the economic cycle, it can be seen that a peak is followed by a recession or a contraction of economic activities, and share prices are likely to tumble. If you invested in overpriced shares during the peak period and share prices subsequently tumbled, you would suffer losses on your investment. Even if you hold on to the shares, it would take a very long time for the share price to go back up to that overvalued price in order for you to sell them at a profit.

Economic recessions have the largest impact on stock market returns (Hamilton & Lin, 1996). Recessions are characterized by an increase in unemployment levels, company closures due to lack of adequate business to sustain company operations, a significant reduction in demand for the company's products, and failure to service debt that was obtained during the recovery stage. If the economic outlook is gloomy, and businesses are struggling, expected cash flows from holding shares are also low, which would lead investors to value shares at a very low price.

The USA has experienced a total of 17 recessions, and

Amadeo (2019) gives a detailed narration in her article on the history of recessions in the United States. From the article, it can be seen that each recession was triggered by different events, an economy can be stuck in a recessionary period for a few months in one recession and a significant number of years in another. For example, in 1857 more than 5,000 businesses went under and the recession lasted 18 months. In 1873, the recession lasted from more than three years, while the Great Depression lasted from 1929 to 1938. In 1907, the stock market dropped by 50% during the recession, which lasted a year.

Given the way that shares lose value during a contraction period, it therefore follows that investors should try to identify a trough, which is the next stage in the economic cycle following a recession. The trough is the bottoming process, i.e. the worst ever of the business cycle, and marks the point just before the economy transitions to recovery.

The stock market tracks the economic cycle, that is, stock market investment performs well when the economy is expanding, and stock market prices fall when the economy is contracting. Thus, as an investor, if you have been tracking the performance of the stock market, and you see stock prices starting to increase, this may signify that the economy is entering the recovery phase, and this may be a good time to buy shares. Shares at this point are likely to be undervalued, and if indeed the economy is in expansion, share prices are likely to continue to go up.

Investor Sentiment

Closely linked to the way the stock market tracks economic cycles is investor sentiment. This sentiment refers to the general prevailing attitude or mood to anticipated price movements on the stock market. If investors are confident that stock prices are going to increase, there is likely to be a surge in the demand for shares, as all investors who have the same sentiment want to buy before the anticipated stock increase so that they lock in their investments at very low prices. But, due to the forces of supply and demand, this surge in the demand of stock is going to result in the prices of stock actually going up.

The opposite also applies. If investors think that stock prices are going to tumble, there is likely to be a number of investors who will try to dispose of their shareholding in order to cash in on capital gains before the anticipated stock price decline happens. And the result? The increase in the number of investors reducing their shareholding actually drives the share price down! This attitude, which drives stock prices, is driven by emotion. Sometimes this emotion is in reaction to news and sometimes stock prices just go up for no reason, e.g. around Christmas.

Technical terms that one is likely to encounter are "bullish market" and "bearish market." A bull or bullish market is one when investor sentiment is positive—investors expect prices to keep rising and they act on this expectation by buying more stocks, resulting in a rise in stock prices. A bear or bearish market, on the other hand, is one where stock prices are expected to decline.

Investor sentiment can, thus, can lead the economic cycle. That is, you can find the stock market changing from bullish to bearish whilst the economy is still in an expansionary phase and is yet to hit the peak period (Pikovsky,

2019). However, there are other investors who chose to take an opposite view, i.e. trade opposite the market. This means when it is a bear market, they choose to invest as if it a bull market, and vice versa.

The bottom line is, investor sentiment is not an exact science. While it shows what the majority of investors think about the general direction of share prices, as an individual investor, your own actions should be informed by information. There could be above average gains, which can be earned from following other investors, but with adequate research and information one can trade opposite the market and still make above-average returns.

Industry Performance

We discussed the business cycle and showed how it affects stock markets. But does this mean that all industries are affected the same way and there is no way that an investor can make returns? The good news is that not all industries perform the same, and an investor can maximize returns by knowing which sectors to invest in with each phase of the business cycle.

Thune (2019) and Pikovsky (2019) break down the recovery or expansion phase into three stages: early-cycle, mid-cycle, and late-cycle. They suggest that

during each phase, investors are better off
concentrating their shareholdings in the following
industries:

es of the Business Cycle	Industry
y-cycle phase	sumer cyclicals, financials, industrials.
-cycle phase	strials, information hology, and basic materials.
-cycle phase (economy ng overheated)	gy, utilities, health care, consumer staples.

...ssion phase	...gy, utilities, health care, consumer staples.

Consumer cyclicals refer to goods and services that are not necessities.   Think of it in this manner: Should your family fall on hard times and you have to tighten the budget, what are the first things that you likely to strike off the budget? For most, things like movie night for the family, where you all go out for an early supper at your favorite restaurant followed by a movie and popcorn, would be among one of the first things to be struck off. What about the monthly mother-daughter shopping visits to the mall to check out new fashion items? Monthly subscriptions to the gym, when you only go once or twice per annum? Your plan to upgrade the TV in the den from 43- inch flat screen to a 55-inch, and then use the 43-inch as a dedicated gaming TV for the boys in the basement? Renovation plans?

I am sure you get the picture. During the recession stage, this kind of expenditure that is likely to be cut off from the budget is also known as discretionary expenditure and gets whittled down to a bare minimum, and companies that specialize in these things are the most affected when the economy is contracting.

During the early-cycle phase, the stock of these companies is at its lowest and this is the best time for a stock investor to buy shares. As the economy expands, business starts to improve and share prices are likely to go up. As an investor, if you bought shares early, you are likely to earn high capital gains on your investment.

Consumer cyclicals can be divided into two categories: durable and non- durable. Just as much as people cannot spend on entertainment, they also can't buy durable goods when their budget does not permit. So, such expenditures are often shelved. The most vulnerable sector to the economic cycle is construction (Pikovsky, 2019). However, this sector is very volatile and very sensitive to changes in the economic cycle, such that when the economy starts to contract, the sector does very poorly.

So, if your stock holding includes such companies, should you then constantly be selling and buying shares depending on the stage of the business cycle? This depends on what kind of stock market investor you are and our objectives. Are you a trader or an investor? Keep in mind that capital gains can only be realized if you actually sell of your shares.
Otherwise, any returns that can be reported on a period by period basis are just paper returns.

For example, imagine you buy shares at $10 per share at the beginning of the year. Share price shoots up to $20 during the first six months, the economy then goes into a recession and the share price steadily drop until it reaches
$9.5 dollars a share. The value of the shares thus fluctuates with the change in the share price, but as long as you keep holding on to the shares, any capital gains or losses that could have been realized are not realized.
However, when the company declares dividends, these dividends are actual returns that you are getting on your investment without having to dispose of the shares.

If at the end of the year you decide to dispose of these shares, despite the price being so low, and in that year, you received a dividend equal to 60¢ per share, would you have made a profit or loss on your investment?

Buying at
$10 per share and selling at $9.50 means that you will
have incurred a loss of 50¢ for each share that you
own. However, the dividend cushions the investor
and reduces the loss. In this case, even though you
would have made capital losses of 50¢ per share, the
dividend cancels out the loss and you are left with an
overall return equal to 10¢ per share.

This example also highlights the importance of
monitoring your portfolio and knowing what's
happening on the stock market instead of just
maintaining a passive approach. Someone else with
the same stock holding could have realized that when
the stock hit $20, if they disposed of their share, they
would lock in a whopping capital gain of $10 per
share after a mere six months! If this is actually acted
on and the capital gains are realized, that investor
would have made a total profit of $10 per share. That
means if they bought 100 shares, the profit would be
$1,000 in 6 months.
What if they had bought 1,000 shares? Their profit
would be $10,000 dollars in just 6 months.

The takeaway from all this is that dividend paying stocks actually lessen the blow from any capital gains losses. But remember, in order to make significant returns, an investor should monitor their portfolio.

In the mid-cycle phase, the consumer staples sector includes makers and traders of food, beverages, tobacco, non-durable household goods, and personal products. Demand for these products is not as responsive to the business cycle. Investing in such companies is likely to yield steady returns, irrespective of whether the economy is at the peak and exhibiting signs of a crisis or in the recession phase. Examples of consumer staples stocks in the USA are Walmart, Conagra, and Kroger.

The health care industry also performs very well when the economy is in a crisis. This is because demand for health care doesn't change with the economic cycle. Not counting elective procedures or surgeries, e.g. plastic surgeries that may be taken to improve appearance (does my nose look a bit crooked?). The need for health care cannot be delayed and therefore there is always a steady demand for health care and pharmaceutical products, which insulates the industry from recessions. Most health care stocks are also dividend stocks, and one can reasonably expect an increase in dividends year in and year out.

Economic Factor That Affect Stock Prices

Inflation and interest rates are economic factors that affect and drive the stock market that an investor should try and understand, whether they are day traders or long-term investors, before investing in the stock market. Knowing this information is going to help the investor understand the value of news and be able to easily process the likely impact on what is happening in the economy on their portfolio.

When it comes to inflation, extremes have a negative impact on the stock market and such figures are not welcomed by investors. When a country is in a hyperinflationary environment, with inflation above 20%, stock prices may keep up at first and give the illusion that the stock market is a good hedge against inflation. However, as the country's currency becomes weak as inflation rate keeps going up, the currency can become worthless. That also means that your portfolio of shares also becomes worthless. Normally, hyperinflation means that the economy is on the verge of collapse, so why invest in the stock market in such an environment?

The other extreme end is deflation. This should be a good sign to investors then, right? Wrong! A deflationary environment is when the general price level of goods is going down. This is worse than inflation because it causes people to hold on to their savings. Think about it: Why spend today when what you want to buy can be bought much cheaper in just a few weeks? A deflationary environment, characterized by a persistent drop in prices, can thus drag an economy into a recession and signals that the economy is not doing well. This causes a drop in the stock market.

The Consumer Price Index (CPI), which compares changes in the price of a basket of goods and services, is thus an important measure that can signal inflation rates in an economy. A healthy dose of inflation is good, the norm is 2% to 3%, and if one wants to invest in the stock market, it must be in an economy where the country has a reign on inflation.

Interest rates are set by the reserve bank and are a tool that is used to reign in on inflation. If inflation is too high, the government raises the interest rate.
High interest rates make borrowing expensive for both businesses and consumers. This dampens spending in

the economy and encourages households to save instead, which mops up excess money supply.

High interest rates have a negative impact on the stock market. The implication is that, as interest rates go up, so does the cost of borrowing. This puts a damper on companies' expansion plans as the cost of capital is prohibitive. Combined with the drop in household demand for goods and services due to a high cost in borrowing, this results in investors not expecting any growth in the earning potential of companies. Therefore, a drop in the stock market occurs.

Low interest rates are associated with an economy that is expanding as access to cheap credit means more spending by both companies and individuals. This means general optimism in company performance which causes the stock market to rally upwards.

These economic fundamentals complement the analysis that was made under economic cycles. When the economy is overheating, that is, when it is at the peak stage of the economic cycle, inflation is very high. This is seen through a constant increase in property prices and rentals, so much so that people generally struggle to afford these things, as salaries are no longer keeping pace with the increase in prices.

An increase in interest rate is also observed during inflationary environments, as was explained above. The stock market starts declining, and in some industries, if it is in a bear market, the stock will already have started losing value long before the economy reached the peak level as investor confidence in the economy wanes. As the economy continues to slide further into recession, lending becomes even riskier and banks demand higher premiums for taking on the additional risk if they are to lend in such an environment.

Another factor that can be analyzed in the same way is unemployment rates. Politics also has an impact on the stock market. Election periods, trade wars with other countries, and so on. But the effect of politics on the stock market is not always intuitive. The best way to understand the possible impact of politics on the stock market is to listen to financial news analysts, who often break down the likely impact on breaking news.

Chapter 3:
The Game of the Mind

Psychological Traits of Successful Investors

Investopedia lists the following as psychological traits of successful investors: optimistic attitude, high self-esteem, high self-worth, a sense of internal power and balance away from the market.

These points may appear abstract and unrelated to trading success, but if you take time to think about it, investors are people. Ordinary people just like you and any other person you can think about—from the richest person in the world with a net worth of billions of dollars to the cocaine junkie who only trades once in a while just to raise money for a quick fix if they have run dry to an unemployed widow whose husband passed on last year and has four little kids to take care of and is trying to invest to secure her babies' futures—the list goes on. And there is a vast spectrum of colorful people who are behind all the liquidity in the stock market and the movement of shares every trading second. There is, however, one undeniable fact: Some investors are more successful in trading the stock than others.

Successful investing in the stock market, in addition to mastering the technique, requires discipline and commitment. Just like going to work, you need to be disciplined and committed enough to set aside time to think about your investment need, develop your investment strategy, read about the stock market and how it works, track the performance of your investment, and so on. The importance and commitment, in the form of time set aside to think and action your investment and to keep trying until you find a winning strategy that works for you and to stick to the money management plan, cannot be overemphasized.

This is not achievable if you have a host of unresolved personal issues and destructive habits that take away your ability to be disciplined and committed. The important point here is that it is not possible to completely separate the professional trader from the person you are. Your personal life will, whether you acknowledge it or not, impact on your ability to trade efficiently and to commit. Think about this: Can one trade efficiently when they are stoned? How about when they are very emotional due to the loss of a loved one? How about when they are very sleepy because they spent the night drinking and partying and they have a really serious hangover?

That said, successful traders, in addition to having a control on their personal issues, also need to have the psychological aptitude to make it. This starts when one believes they can do this. Scary as it may be, investing in the stock market is not for a certain class of people whom you may imagine are the privileged ones in society. It's for anyone who has high
self-esteem, high self-worth, and a sense of internal power to believe that they can change their personal circumstances by standing up and making things happen.

The whole point of investment is to try and make

positive returns. While this may be so, there are a lot of external factors, that an investor has no control over. These factors may determine whether any applied strategy, no matter how well researched, works or doesn't work. Despite this knowledge, as an investor, you don't have total control and can't guarantee positive results all the time since losses are part of the game.

Only optimistic people, who believe that this is possible, will find it in them to be disciplined and to commit time and resources to try and try again until they strike gold. If you are very pessimistic and don't think that there are any returns at all that can be made from investing in stocks, then stock investing is not for you! However, true life stories of ordinary people who managed to amass wealth can be found on the internet if you are skeptical or you need inspiration whenever you feel discouraged.

Potential Psychological Pitfalls

When one thinks of an investor, the image that is conjured up is a rational thinking individual who has the intellectual abilities to gather relevant information at little or no cost, analyze it, and then use it to make logical investment decisions in return for rewards. All the while taking into account their risk appetite and abilities to manage that risk. Most finance models assume that all investors fit this ideal type that is described.

However, there is a branch of economics that acknowledges that, in practice, some of these assumptions may not necessarily be true. Some investors suffer from errors of perception and judgment which may cause an investor to make bad investment decisions that result in losses. While this may be bad for the investor concerned, it may create opportunities to make profit for those who are geared to take advantage of pricing errors on the market.

Ritholtz (2005) lists six common errors of perception in judgment. These are: overconfidence, fear of regret, cognitive dissonance, anchoring, representativeness, and myopic risk aversion. These errors are discussed below, and it is important for the beginner investor to be aware of this before they venture into stock investing so that they don't fall into the same pit that others have unknowingly found themselves in.

Overconfidence

Overconfidence in one's abilities as an investor and overconfidence in the reliability of information. And the result? Overconfidence leads to more frequent trading, even when this trading is based on wrong information. The end result is, more often than not, lower return. To avoid falling into this trap, investors should trade less. They should also pay attention to historical price information instead of basing investment decisions wholly on beliefs about future outcomes.

Fear of Regret

The fear of making a wrong decision, and how an investor will then feel if this happens, can paralyze an investor. This fear of regret manifests itself in the form of procrastination: delaying making decisions as much as possible and hesitating a lot when the decision can no longer be postponed. As a result, an investor may lose out on chances to make profitable returns due to this paralysis. Typical investors then hold on to stocks for far too long, even though they are seeing that they made a bad investment and the stock is losing value. They also sell stocks that are gaining in value far too early due to the fear that, if they delay selling, the stock price may fall. The end result is lower than optimal returns.

The lesson from all this information is: If you bet on stock to move in a certain direction but it doesn't— don't hold on to it. Acknowledge that you made an error and cut off your losses as soon as possible. This discipline will also be applied with winning stocks and you won't sell too soon, resulting in an improvement in investment returns.

Cognitive Dissonance

Have you ever walked into a shop and bought something then you feel like kicking yourself because you're no longer sure if buying it was a wise decision? This feeling is made worse by seeing other competitive brands, and the natural response to lessen this feeling will be to avoid any information pertaining to competitive products. You will only look at information relating to the product that you bought in a bid to convince yourself that you made the right decision.

That is called cognitive dissonance. This same phenomenon is also found among stock market investors. Sometimes after buying certain stocks, you may start getting conflicting information that calls into question your decision to buy.

So, what should an investor do? Instead of avoiding this information, the best thing is to re-evaluate the basis on which the decision to buy was based on. If indeed the reasons used to inform the buy decision no longer hold,
e.g. the stock price has gone down when you expected it to go up, the best

thing to do would be to acknowledge that buying was a bad investment call. You should act by disposing of the stock before losing a lot of money.

Anchoring

These are "decision-making errors from mental shortcuts that are a normal part of the way we think," (Ritholtz, 2005). Instead of doing a complete analysis to determine the value of a share, an investor would typically use historical prices as cues for whether a share is overvalued or undervalued.

A stock that was trading at a higher price in the past that has now fallen to a new price level would typically be taken as cheap, and an investor would make a purchasing decision based on this thought process. However, it is actually a bad buy, which was just overvalued on the market because most investors were holding onto the share.

The fall in price might be the market correcting itself. Investors should thus avoid making decisions based on incomplete information as seen through the use of limited characteristics.

Myopic Risk Aversion

This is when investors are preoccupied with the

performance of their portfolio in the short-term, such that they miss the long-term benefits of investing in the stock market. If an investor pays too much attention to short-term volatility, this preoccupation may lead an investor to invest more of their savings in less risky options, like treasury bills, and less in stocks.
This is done even though stocks provide a higher return in the long run.

As an investor, access to too much information may stress you too much and may result in you poring over price sheets after every hour, despite your investment goals, which do not require you to do so if you are not a day trader. To avoid doing this, pick out your investments well, and take it easy on calculating your potential returns every hour.

Chapter 4: Important Things You Need to Know About Stocks, Options, and Forex

This book is primarily about investing in the stock market, but that is not the only investment option that an investor should think about. The concept of diversifying, or spreading investments, amongst different assets to minimize risk can cushion you, as an investor, through minimizing risk while maximizing returns. In order to appreciate all investment options that can complement investment in the stock market, this section details important features about stocks, options, and forex.

Stocks

This section examines some of the small, but important, issues that an investor needs to be aware of before investing. It was highlighted in a previous chapter that individuals can only invest in the stock exchange via a broker. Brokers require a minimum initial deposit in order to start trading, which means that you cannot run away from saving first before you start trading in stocks.

The amount of money you need is ultimately dependent on the broker you choose to use. There is no minimum number of shares that one can buy. You can buy as little as one share or even fractional shares. High-value shares, like Berkshire Hathaway's share, is currently selling at over $295,000 per share and is the most expensive share in the world. Other expensive shares are Seaboard Corporation, trading above $3,500 per share, and NVR Incorporated, trading at over $2,400 per share. Due to the high costs, some brokerages and investment companies allow their clients to buy fractions of such shares.

As a beginner investor, it is important to note that you are not limited to trading low valued shares. You can also have access to these high valued shares and can trade them if you have access to the right trading platforms. Examples of such investment companies are Betterment, Stash, and Stockpile. But whatever you decide to do, you have to keep in mind that with every transaction that goes through a broker, there are transactional costs that have to be paid.

Some brokers charge a flat fee every month and some have a commission- based charge that depends on the value of the transaction. This means that even though, theoretically, there is no minimum number of shares, in order for the trades to generate enough profit to cover transaction costs, there is a minimum number that one needs to purchase for trading to be viable.
Depending on your capital, you should buy blocks of shares between
$500-$1,000.

Market hours for trading stocks are between 9:30 a.m. and 4 p.m. However, the best times to trade shares is when volume and volatility is high, and that is usually within the first hour the market opens and an hour before the market closes.

In order to make it easy to sharpen your trading strategy, you can start by just trading a few stocks, or start by just trading one stock. If you do this, you will understand the stock, the factors that drive the stock price, and you are thus able to pre-empt how certain news is likely to impact the stock without having to research a lot. As you get more and more comfortable, you can then look at other stocks within the industry. With time, you can widen your trading strategy to include other stocks until you have a fairly well diversified portfolio.

To place a trade, a distinction has to be made between market orders and limit orders. A market order happens when you choose to execute the trade instantaneously at the prevailing market price. While with a limit order, it is a conditional trade. You get to specify that you wish to buy the stock if the price drops to a certain level or you wish to sell the stock if the price increases to a certain level.

Since individuals can only trade through a broker, the choice of the broker you use can be one of the harrowing decisions faced by a beginner trader. Other important factors to consider are the availability of a free demo account to practice before you start trading live, minimum account balances that are within your savings range, clear commission and brokerage fee charges, tutorials and other educational content to help you get started, and access to security analysis tools.

Conducting all this broker research in addition to all the other investor related information you need to figure out can be overwhelming. However, there are quite a number of analysts who conduct this kind of review, and a simple google site on the best online stockbrokers can yield useful results. Some sights rank broker using various criteria that may or may not be exactly in line with what you consider as the most attractive features in a brokerage firm. You should also look at reviews from other clients before you finally make a choice of which broker you want to use.

Options

Options are derivative instruments whose value and profit derives from the value of an underlying instrument, which could be stocks, stock indexes, currencies, commodities, or bonds. That said, an option is a contract that gives you the right, but not the obligation, to buy or sell an underlying asset at a predetermined price. There are two types of options: American options and European options, whose distinction is based on when the contract can be exercised. An American option can be exercised any time before the agreed date known as the expiration date whilst a European can only be exercised on the expiration date.

As an investor, you can use options to speculate about the price movements of the underlying asset. But these contracts can also be used to arrange the delivery or receipt of the underlying asset and to hedge against losses on other positions in the underlying asset. An option buyer has to pay an option premium, and this value depends on the volatility of the underlying asset and the market. If the underlying asset or the broad market is more volatile, then the premium that has to be paid is also high.

There are two types of options: put options and call options. With each option, there are two parties, known as the option buyer and the option seller. The value of options declines. One of the factors that influence this decay is time, with options becoming of less worth as the time to expiration approaches. Options are not as liquid as other investment assets, and their pricing uses the mathematical Black Scholes model which can be difficult to understand for the average investor.

Futures

An alternate way to make money is to trade physical goods like oil. If you are always able to buy low and sell high, or sell high and buy low, you will always make a profit. For example, if you expect the price of oil to go up, you should enter into a contract that allows you to buy barrels of oil today at a price agreed upon today. If at the maturity of the contract it turns out you were right, and the price of oil has indeed gone up, it means you have made a profit on my trade.

The difference between the current price of oil and the contract price multiplied by the barrels of oil is your profit. But if you think about it, there are other costs that may make this strategy unprofitable. For instance, how will you transport the oil? How will you store it? Will you need insurance to make sure you don't lose my goods, e.g. insure against theft, fire, and all the other ways goods can be damaged? And when the price has gone up for you to sell, who should bear the transport costs? Will you still be having any profit after covering all these costs?

A futures contract allows investors to trade based on the price movement of commodities like gold, oil, wheat, etc. without having to buy and sell the physical goods. As such, a futures contract on gold or wheat doesn't necessarily mean that the investor will ever get to take delivery of gold or wheat.

There are always two parties to a futures contract, one investor who wants to sell the commodity and the other who wants to buy the commodity. So, when you are investing, you have to choose whether you are going short, which means you are agreeing to sell the underlying commodity, or you are going long, which means you are agreeing to buy the underlying commodity at an agreed future date at a price that is agreed to at the present moment.

Let's assume you go long. At the end of the contract period, if the price has indeed risen, the other party to the contract (the one who agreed to sell) has to pay you the difference between the agreed price and the current price per barrel of oil. Why? If you insist on settling the contract, you would expect the one in the short position to physically deliver the barrels of oil that you bought at the low price that you agreed on, and then you will sell the oil at the higher market price, making a profit equal to (current market per barrel less contract price per barrel) the number of oil barrels bought.

This is the same profit that you would have been making if you had actually purchased the physical barrels of oil and kept them in a warehouse somewhere. Then, when the price had risen enough, decided to sell them on the open market. But the difference is that there are no transaction costs, you can trade with anyone on the stock exchange, which makes futures contacts very liquid. The exchange regulates all contracts and you, therefore, don't have to worry about default, inspecting the physical goods to determine grade and/or quality, contract sizes, etc.

All futures contracts are exchange-traded contracts which are highly regulated and standardized as follows:

Each contract represents a standard weight or fixed measure: Delivery and payment terms. Quality/grade.

It is important to note that each exchange formulates the contract terms that are traded, and therefore, futures contract terms for the same commodity, though traded in different exchanges, can be different. Information on future contracts that are tradeable in an exchange is available on the exchange website.

Forex

The forex market (foreign exchange market or FX) is just like a stock exchange, with the only difference being that instead of buying and selling shares of a company, investors buy and sell currencies. The price that is used is the foreign exchange rate, which is the price that one currency is stated in terms of another currency.

For example, if you are in South Africa and you need US dollars to pay for a car that you intend to import, you would have to convert a certain amount of rands to get US dollars. One rand, as of October 2019, buys 0.069 US dollars. Someone else in the UK, who also wants to buy US dollars, would be paying one pound to get 1.29 US dollars.

This amount of money that one will get in exchange for a unit of the domestic currency is called the exchange rate. As can be seen from the example given, some currencies are stronger than other currencies. Some of the most liquid currencies are the US dollar, British pound, Japanese yen, and the euro. Banks, investment managers, multinational corporations, and investors are some of the participants who invest in forex markets.

Forex markets exist as cash markets as well as derivative markets where currency swaps and other derivative instruments used to hedge forex positions are bought and sold. Forex trading happens electronically over the counter markets in the major financial centers 24 hours a day and investor can choose to participate in either spot markets, also called cash markets, forward markets, and futures markets.

Reasons for trading forex are varied, but include speculative trades where traders try to make profits from the movement in exchange rates whilst corporations trade currencies to conduct international business. The forex market is attractive to most individual investors because one does not need a lot of capital to start trading. There is also a lot of flexibility in trading as there are active markets around the clock, which enables some individuals to trade outside working hours as a way of making extra money.

Most brokers offer demo accounts that provide investors who are new to trading an opportunity to practice in a simulated environment before they start trading live. As such, as a beginner investor, you can practice different trading strategies, like day trading and swing trading, until you are confident of the trading strategy that works for you before moving to a live environment. Brokers also offer the use of leverage, which can amplify profits, but this should be used with caution as it can also amplify losses and result in a depletion of invested capital.

There is also a lot of currency pairs that one can invest in and high liquidity in the market which promotes efficient pricing. However, in trading, investors should be aware of high brokerage costs and should understand brokerage charges and commissions charged for services. It is important not to enter the forex market blindly, you should have adequate knowledge about what drives forex markets and how to trade profitably.

Bonds

Bonds are usually touted as an essential part of any retirement investment portfolio. Imagine an investment that is not likely to lose any money if held to maturity, irrespective of what happens to the economy. It provides a steady stream of income, is liquid enough for an investor to liquidate should the investor need the capital and can also provide tax-free income. So, how can one invest in these bonds?

To invest in bonds is to lend money to a corporation, government, or municipality for a certain period. In exchange for this loan, you are guaranteed interest payments, also known as coupons, that are payable either quarterly, semiannually, or annually. At the end of the investment period, you then get back the money that you invested at the beginning, which is known as the principal or face value. This type of investment thus offers a stable periodic income. As such, if the investor intends to hold the bond until maturity, the investment is likely to be insulated from volatility.

The investor will know right from the outset the return that they are committing to, and if all expected cash flows are received, the expected return will be exactly equal to the realized return.

When compared to dividend stocks, bonds are less volatile since common stock dividends that are declared are dependent on profits that are made in each financial year. The investor also cannot predict the value of the share at the end of their invest period with certainty. Most of the return for stocks comes from capital gains, while with bonds, most of the return comes from interest payments. As such, if the bonds are to be held to maturity, they are a good investment for someone who intends to cover a known liability in the future when compared to stocks.

Bonds are liquid instruments that can be traded on a secondary market. Due to the diversity of issued bonds, bonds are traded in over the counter markets, unlike stocks, which are traded on exchanges. There are different types of bonds that one can invest in, and some of these are:

Treasury bonds

These are issued by the government to finance its budget deficits and as part of monetary policy tools that are used to manage money supply in an economy. They are low risk since a government is ordinarily not expected to default on its obligations. As a result, return is always lower than other higher risk bonds. These bonds, however, perform better than other higher risk bonds when the economy is in a recession.

Municipal bonds

The yield on these bonds is usually low, but all interest payments are exempt from income taxes.

Corporate bonds

These can further be subdivided into high quality, investment grade bonds, and high yield corporate bonds are also known as junk bonds. All bonds that are issued by corporations are rated by rating agencies like Standard and Poor, Moody's Investor Service, and Fitch Ratings. This rating is a letter that is assigned to a bond. For example, Standard and Poor uses the following rating system:

AAA: Lowest risk.
AA: Low risk.

A: Low risk.
BBB: Medium risk.
BB, B: High risk.
CCC, CC, C: Highest risk.
D: In default.

The rating that is attached to a bond signifies the credit quality of the bond and considers the issuer's ability to pay the periodic coupons and principal when its due. This rating, since it highlights the risk inherent in the bond, influences the return that investors may want to be compensated. So, obviously, low risk bonds offer lower yields while higher risk bonds offer higher yields.

Foreign bonds

With these bonds, the issuer promises to make fixed interest payments and to pay back the principal in currency. The prevailing exchange rate determines the payment that eventually flows to the investors. As such, performance is highly dependent on the exchange rate.

Secured bond

With these bonds, the issuer pledges a specific asset as collateral to guarantee against default. Should the issuer default, the title of the assets passes on to the bondholders and the assets will be sold to cover the outstanding obligations.

Console bond

This is a bond with no maturity date. The coupon payments thus represent a perpetual income stream, and the issuer is not expected to redeem it. If, as an investor, you bought a console, the only way to recover your investment is to sell it on the secondary market.

Stock Splits

There are some shares which, due to high demand on the market, end up being very expensive. Take for example the stocks of Berkshire Hathaway, which as of February 2019 were trading above $305,000 shares. Seaboard Corporation trades above $3,600 per share, and NVR Incorporated trades at above $2,400 per share. How many investors can afford to bid for such shares on the exchange? And in what quantities? Also, as an investor, if you now want to sell your shares, how easy is it?

As a corporation grows bigger and more profitable, it begins to attract more and more investors. Its share price is likely to be bid up, which is what provides high capital gains to investors who are able to do value investing,
i.e. identifies companies with high potential and invests in them before the share price skyrockets.

In order to boost liquidity in such high-value shares, existing stocks are thus split. This has the impact of reducing the values of the shares without changing the market capitalization of the company.

Since all public companies have a set value of shares that are outstanding, the board of directors can increase the number of shares outstanding by issuing more shares to current shareholders. The terminology that is used is a 2-for-1 stock split.

A 2-for-1 stock split means that for every share that is owned by a holder, they have received an additional one and they now have two shares. If, as an investor, you owned 20 shares, after the stock split, you will have 40 shares. Market capitalization still remains the same, which means that the share price has been effectively been halved.

Existing shareholder usually benefit from stock splits. This is because when the market value per share goes down, investors who have always wanted to invest in such share, but couldn't because of the high share value, are now able to bid for the shares. The increase in demand is thus likely to push the share price up after the initial drop, and existing shareholders are able to cash in on capital gains.

Chapter 5:
Stock Markets, Functionalities, and Factors That Influence Them

Every country has a stock market, and the performance of the stock market is correlated with how the economy is performing. For example, when an economy is expanding, and companies are recording profits, the share prices on the stock exchange of such companies also go up. This is also in part due to households having more disposable income and more savings that they can use to invest.

An index is a tool that measures change. A stock market index, therefore, is a tool that measures how all companies, grouped into similar stocks, have performed in a certain period. Stocks that are listed on an exchange are grouped using market capitalization, industry, and geographical segment. Any change in the value of the individual stocks affects the total value of the index, and it is thus possible to tell how the market as a whole has been performing.

Investors cannot invest directly in an index, but these indexes are used as benchmarks when creating diversified portfolios by maintaining the weights of stocks in the index. They are also used as benchmarks when determining how investments are performing. The percentage change in the index over time is what conveys information that is useful to investors, not the index number itself. Most mutual funds try to provide investors with exposure to a given market by attempting to trek a particular index. As such, investors get built-in diversification and a predictable return if the fund is able to mimic the index they are tracking.

There are a number of different indexes that are generally used. However, each index is only made up of certain stocks that meet a set criterion and therefore do not represent the whole market. The implication of this to the individual investor is that even though indexes show the general movement in the market, it might have no impact on the stocks that you are interested in investing in. If the index is down, you may still see individual stock prices going up and actually make huge capital gains despite the index being down.

The information that is conveyed by indexes is also historical since it reflects trades that have already happened. So, they are useful in showing trends. Some of the most popular indexes are the S&P 500, Dow Jones, and NASDAQ.

Indexes

S&P 500

This index includes 500 of the most widely traded stocks on stock exchanges in the United States. It is a market capitalization weighted index that represents 70% of the total market value and is the most inclusive index. Most major brokers and investment companies offer funds that mimic the index that investors can buy into.

Dow Jones

This is a price weighted index that is composed of 30 stocks of the largest, and most influential, companies in the US and represents one quarter of the total market value. Despite it having only 30 stocks, it is a good indicator of general market trends in the US. An investor can invest in the Dow by buying shares in the companies that are listed on the Dow. There are also several exchange traded funds that track the index.

NASDAQ

A significant number of listed companies on the

NASDAQ stock market are within the technology sector, followed by the financial industry. Other industries that are included are consumer services, health care, consumer durables, amongst others. These companies are of different sizes, industries, and regions of the world. The NASDAQ market has two indexes: the NASDAQ Composite and the NASDAQ 100. The composite index includes all the stocks that are listed on the NASDAQ market, while the NASDAQ 100 tracks the largest 100 stocks, excluding those in the financial industry.

Foreign Markets

One way of getting access to foreign markets is to invest in exchange traded funds that hold international bonds and stocks. Exchange traded funds are a pooled form of investment that hold a basket of international stocks and bonds which are passively managed.

The funds are set to track a certain index and thus benefit investors through exposing them to that markets' returns. The fund allows for more diversification as it can invest in a lot of assets, including commodities.

To invest in these, an investor can buy units by either paying a lump sum of money or through a series of payments. These funds are traded like shares on exchanges and are thus very liquid. Since they are exchange traded, some investors prefer to actively manage their investment by buying and selling their share.

These funds are getting increasingly more attractive to investors all over the world because investors have realized that actively managed funds rarely beat the market. Passively managed funds, like the exchange traded funds, thus have very low management costs, which boosts overall return. This makes them one of the best investment options for retirement funds. There are some funds that are leverages, and these offer investors the chance to earn returns that are higher than the index they track.

Chapter 6: Strategies for Beginners

This section details strategies that can be employed by a beginner trader on the stock exchange. That said, please note that these strategies cannot be fully understood just from reading about them. It is important to practice and try to implement them before you invest your money. Most brokers provide dummy trading platforms which can be used by beginner traders to practice their chosen trading strategies and refine their investment goals.

It's one thing to choose to define yourself as a day trader or a swing trader based on literature that you have read. But in practice, you may find that day trading is not compatible with you. The quick returns that people think can actually be reaped are a result of long working hours, a commitment to self-teaching without any guidance, and risk-taking abilities.

For example, an investor may not have the time to be a day trader as he/she will be at work during stock exchange opening hour. That said, the strategy that will be eventually chosen depends on the investor's personality and personal circumstances as they affect the investor's availability, risk tolerance level, and amount of capital that one has as a cushion against losses.

Roth IRA

A Roth IRA is a retirement savings account that allows an investor to withdraw their savings tax-free. Anyone with a taxable income can invest in such funds. The amount of money that can be deposited into a Roth IRA is determined by the IRS, but this is only limited to the earnings from your day job. So, you cannot be allowed to invest in rental income or profits from other businesses, which makes this fund ideal for beginner investors who are trying to build their wealth from their day jobs.

Contribution to this investment account are non-tax deductible. While this may seem like an upfront cost, the investor benefits in the future since all withdrawals will be tax-free. This investment is likely to be more advantageous to individuals who are likely to have higher taxes at retirement.

It is very easy to invest in Roth IRAs as a beginner as all brokerage firms, and most banks and investment companies, offer this investment. As a contributor to a Roth IRA, you have a list of investment options that you can choose from, which include exchange-traded funds and stocks. Within these investment options, you can then choose whether you want to be an active or passive investor.

Though, there is a five-year rule that has to be adhered to for an investor not to be charged tax.

Invest What You Won't Need Soon

The worst thing that you can do as a beginner investor is to start your investment journey with money that you are going to need, like your monthly rent or school fees. If you do this, then you will not be any different from an addicted gambler in a casino, who is betting their all their money, including their transport money home, in the hope that they will make it big one time.

Bear in mind as you embark on your trading journey that this is a learning process, and just like any learner, you will be tested time and time again with every decision you make. Success does not happen overnight, and through this learning journey, a few hard lessons are likely to be learnt— largely through investments gone wrong. With this in mind, investing money that you are likely to need to use soon will further complicate your learning journey for the following reasons:

- **Stock market investment returns typically accrue over time:** How much time generally depends on how well the economy is performing and also the influence of the economic cycle. If your aim is to get returns from capital accumulation as seen through an increase in the share price, then you need to appreciate that this may not happen overnight, or in a week, or two.

In between, as other investors go about implementing their own trading strategies, the stock price may be going up and down. But if you've got the fundamentals right and there is a reasonable expectation that the stock price will go up, only time can work its magic. If you don't have time as an investor, then you may be forced to sell before you have realized the expected returns.

- **The pressure to do well:** Stock markets are, by their very nature, volatile. The more liquid a stock is, then the more volatile it is likely to be, and you are going to observe significant dips and peaks in the share price of invested stocks.

This short-run volatility is normal, but if you are under pressure to do well, chances are that you will be following the performance of your investment with a hawk's eye, with your heart skipping a beat or two every time the stock dips. You will stress even more when the price increases, wondering if that's the best time to exit your position or hold your breath a few minutes longer in the hope of a higher price?

This kind of approach to trading is emotionally draining, tiresome, and so stressful that it may put you off trading. It is certainly not a sustainable model and might increase your medical costs as it can trigger panic attacks and other stress related health conditions.

• **It does not allow you to develop a trading strategy:** A trading strategy is a detailed plan on how you intend to achieve profits in the form of investment returns. There is a difference between thinking about your trading plan theoretically and the one you will end up using.

Remember the components of a trading plan? You will have to define the kind of stocks that you will be trading, entry and exit points, and, most importantly, money management rules. That said, this theoretical trading strategy has to be first converted into a practical one and may need to be fine-tuned and personalized for it to suit you. You will need to take into account the time that you have to actively manage your portfolio, your appetite for risk, your ability to handle stress as the stock market does its thing, and so on.

If, as you are still trying to figure out these things (which you can never find in a textbook by the way), and you suddenly need to exit all your positions because you now need the money, but the timing violates the exit points as set out in the trading strategy, you may never get to figure out what works for you. You try it again the following month, when you get your next paycheck. But what if you have to exit again because your bills are due? This may go on endlessly until you give up despite having been on to a winning trading strategy.

- **It forces you to speculate on the stock market:** There is a difference between investing and speculating in the stock market. Investing is applying funds in the long-term in stocks that have moderate risk by a cautious and conservative investor. Decisions on which stocks to buy are based on fundamentals which are gathered through research in a bid to understand the stock and the market itself. Speculation, on the other hand, is largely based on individual opinion after studying technical charts, and such investors are typically aggressive in their approach as they try to lock in abnormally high short-term gains due to movements in share prices.

Speculation is highly risky as a lot of factors can converge and force the price to move in the opposite direction. If you are using funds that you know are due soon, an attempt to research market fundamentals is likely to be rushed and you may end up investing in the wrong stocks based on incomplete information.

Passive Investment

To be passive means accepting what others do without active response or resistance. If you are a passive investor, the implication from this definition is that you invest in something and then you don't do anything in response to any of the numerous factors that may affect the value of your investment. But does that mean that you can just invest in any stock randomly picked from a price list and you close your eyes, hold your breath, and just hope that you make money? No!

Passive investing is a strategy that enables an investor to maximize returns whilst minimizing actively managing the portfolio through buying and selling. In other words, this is a buy and hold strategy. Whether you are employing a passive or active strategy, the goal with any strategy is to make positive returns.

Passive investors do not seek to benefit from short term fluctuations in the market, rather their portfolio is grown gradually over time. Typical investments that are ideal for passive investments are real estate investment trusts, dividend stocks and index funds.

In order for the buy and hold strategy to work, there

are key rules that have to be followed if a passive investor is to make positive returns.

- **Long investment period:** This is a strategy that is only suitable for investors with a long-term investment horizon. This investment horizon refers to the total length of time that an investor intends to keep their funds locked up in the investment. Investment horizons range from short-term to long-term. A short-term investment horizon typically does not exceed three years, whilst a medium-term horizon means an investment horizon between three years and 10 years, and a long-term investment horizon is above 10 years. So, you do not have funds that you can keep locked up in an investment for at least a decade, then a passive investment strategy may not be ideal for you.

A long investment horizon enables an investor to invest in more risky assets. The reason behind this is that more risk implies a potential for higher returns, but with equity, this return may take time to be accumulated. So, investors with a low appetite for risk are likely to have a short investment horizon and avoid this buy and hold strategy. Those with a high-risk appetite, however, need a long investment horizon to allow their portfolio to recover in the event that the portfolio does not do well in the short run.

• **Income needs:** An investor should define their income needs before choosing an investment strategy. Ask yourself when you are likely to need the funds. Are you investing for retirement and will need the funds in 35 years? Or are you setting up a college fund for your child that you will need in 3 years' time? Your income need thus determines your investment horizon, which in turn determines the investment strategy that an investor is likely to adopt.

• **Risk and diversification:** Passive investing attempts to replicate market returns, and this is usually achieved through investing in highly diversified portfolios. Diversification is a risk management strategy that minimizes the risk of a portfolio by including a variety of assets. If one is investing in the stock market, for example, investing in one stock means you are taking on a lot of risks. If the stock does well, you are going to have positive returns, but if the stock price dips for some reason, you will lose a significant chunk of your investment.

For a buy and hold strategy to work, that means the overall portfolio risk has to be minimized. Each of the individual assets in the portfolio may be risky, but when combined into a portfolio, the overall result will be minimal risk. Some stocks do very well when the economy is in recovery, and the price drops significantly when the economy is contracting. But when these stocks are combined with other stocks that post below-average returns when the economy is recovering. and do well when the economy is in a recession, the overall risk on the portfolio is minimized.

As some stocks lose value on the exchange, the other stocks will be rallying and vice versa. Since a passive investment is associated with well-diversified portfolios, the return is usually an average return. The strategy does not generate large returns that can make a person wealthy overnight but provides an average return that can steadily grow a portfolio.

The benefits of passive investing are numerous, but key amongst these is simplicity. Any beginner investor can just choose an index fund or a group of indexes that are already well-diversified and earn passive returns without having to engage in research or actively managing their portfolio. Passive investing is also associated with low fees since the investor is not constantly buying and selling shares and being charged a commission for every transaction.

However, passive investing limits an investor to a very narrow set of investment assets that are suitable for the buy and hold strategy. Thus, it does not give you, as an investor, a chance to experiment and learn as you go until you discover a winning formula that works for you. The strategy also offers smaller potential returns compared to other trading strategies.

Value Investment

In this strategy, investors invest in undervalued companies, which they identify after conducting thorough fundamental analysis, and hold on to them in the hope that they will make huge capital gains in the future. Take, for example, an investment into a company that has good prospects, but is not yet well established, and as such has shares that are trading at a very low price. Investing in that company now, means you are betting that the company will do well at some point in the future and you are buying in on the large future earnings that the company is likely to make in the future.

For the company to get to that point, it will take time; years, if not decades. In those years, it is likely that as the company is growing, it may not be able to pay dividends as it will be reinvesting most of its earnings. So, as an investor, you won't be earning any returns. Furthermore, as the economy dips and peaks, the share price may also go down in some periods, making it impossible for an investor to pull out of the investment.

Only after the company has made it or is showing unmistakable signs that it is a successful company, such as paying a consistent dividend for example, will it attract attention from other investors. The increase in demand for the stock is then likely to push up the price on the stock market. As the stock rallies, investors who invested early are likely to make huge returns, which may turn into millions of dollars, just from taking on high risk.

Most successful investors, like Warren Buffet, make money from value investing. On the surface, it may look like value investing is similar to passive investment. Afterall, one makes money through buying stock and holding it until the value goes up, but the strategy is not the same and there are key differences.

Effort is applied in identifying companies to be invested in. With value investing, only undervalued stocks are of interest. The investor will sift through all listed stocks, looking for those which meet a select criterion in terms of price/earnings ratios. The investor then rigorously studies each business and tries to forecast its performance in the future by looking at its competitive advantages. If the investor is confident that the business has good prospects and is likely to perform well in the future, which would lead to an increase in the share price, then an investment is made.

In order for such a prediction to be made, the investor has to have a thorough understanding of the business that they are buying into, which implies that a lot of effort goes into stock screening. One factor is a consistent operating history and favorable long-term prospects, as seen through fundamental earning power and good management. Another factor is a consistent operating history and favorable long-term prospects, as seen through fundamental earning power and good management.

The investor also has to keep in mind that the performance of a business is highly dependent on management drive. Companies that are run by managers who are focused on long-term growth and a creation of shareholder wealth are likely to do well compared to those run by managers who only have short-term goals.

There are other factors as well that should be considered before a company is chosen, but the point that should be appreciated is that identifying value companies is not an easy and straightforward process. An investor should have the time to conduct thorough research before committing. This is important because value investors more often than not go against the market. In other words, they believe that from the intensive research conducted, they have superior information that other investors do not have, which will explain why the stock is currently undervalued.

To make the most returns, value investors do not worry much about diversification and are prepared to risk significant chunks of their capital through buying lots of shares of just one stock. As such, this a high-risk investment strategy that is likely to yield high returns.

Chapter 7: Learn from the Pros

If you are still on the fence about whether it's worth it to learn how to invest in the stock market, and what you need to do to be a successful investor, you should read about some of the most successful investors in the world.
Their stories are likely to motivate you and make you realize that some people are not born into money but work hard to make it—from humble beginnings to being billionaires.

A notable point that stands out is that you should keep in mind as you read this chapter is that most of the self-made richest people on earth did not make most of their money by holding 9 a.m. to 5 p.m. day jobs. They made money through investing! This section profiles some of the most successful investors who cracked it and are now some of the richest people in the world.

Warren Buffet

He is one of the richest men on earth, with an estimated net worth of over 40 billion dollars! Buffet owns Berkshire Hathaway, a company that invests in other companies. Most of his money was acquired through value investing, which, as you now know, is the opposite of scouting the market for quick gains.

What sets him apart from other investors is that he takes time to study a company before he makes the decision to invest. Investing in businesses that he understands enables him to correctly predict the impact of news on his investments, as he would have done a full fundamental analysis and be aware of each of his companies' sources of value.

Coca-Cola, Walt Disney, and American Express are some of the biggest brands that Buffet has invested in. With these companies, his strategy was to look for consistent operating history and favorable long-term prospects, as seen through fundamental earning power and good management.

Buffet applies an aggressive strategy to consolidate his shareholding. For instance, he put one-third of all his assets into Coca-Cola, which means he doesn't bother with diversifying as long as he is sure he has identified a good stock to invest in. This kind of investing strategy is however not easily replicable by investors who don't have a huge capital base and the resources to conduct full fundamental analysis.

Benjamin Graham

Benjamin Graham was an intellectual and professional investor who invented security analysis and mentored other notable investors like Warren Buffet in value investing at Columbia Business school. He believes that return is usually linked to the intellectual effort an investor is willing to apply. Such investment strategies and the associated effort that an investor would have to apply were summarized by Serenity Stocks (2012) as follows:

Buying blue chips or index funds is a low effort strategy. Blue chips are well-performing large public companies with well-established and steady dividend policies. Index investing is a passive investment strategy where funds are invested in a fund that mimics a given market. Typically, such funds are well diversified and have low risk and consistent return, albeit low. This strategy applies zero effort and, as a result, returns from this investment strategy rarely beat the market.

If one decides to invest in defensive grade stocks, which are companies with good fundamentals which are priced low by the market, returns will be slightly higher than maintaining a passive strategy. Effort that has to be applied in this case is identifying defensive stocks, and from those, picking those that are not overvalued. Low effort is applied in applying this strategy. This results in returns that are a bit higher than the passive strategy applied above.

Another strategy is investing in enterprising grade stocks, which requires medium effort. Enterprising stocks are not as well established as defensive stocks. As a result, an investor has to apply effort in identifying such stocks and in diversifying their portfolio as these stocks are riskier.

The last strategy, which requires maximum effort, is investing in net current asset value per share (NCAV) grade stocks. These are stocks that sell for less than the value of their cash worth and with positive earnings in the last year. An investor has to put in a lot of effort in identifying such shares. In addition, they have to make sure the portfolio they create with such stocks is well diversified with at least 30 stocks. This an active investment strategy as effort is required in the selection, verification, tracking, and balancing of the component stock. If one is able to achieve all this, they will make very high profits.

George Soros

Founder and chairman of Soros Fund Management with a net worth of 8 billion dollars, George Soros has a trading strategy that is markedly different from the one applied by Warren Buffet. Picking the right advisor, taking a trial and error approach, keeping emotions out of investment picks, and being bold and going all out if you believe you are making the right decisions are some of the guiding principles that have earned him billions of dollars.

In short, Soros is a speculative investor and mainly profits from short-term volatility and highly leveraged investment deals. Fundamental analysis when applying this trading strategy is of little value. Day traders are likely to learn much from analyzing his trading strategies as they specialize in betting on the market to make high returns in the shortest possible time.

Raymond Dalio

Dalio is a successful investor who runs one of the most successful hedge funds in the world: Bridgewater Associates. He is also one of the richest men, with a net worth above 18 billion dollars.

His hedge fund was started in 1975, but long before that he was an active investor. He believes in technical analysis as a tool that can aid investors in making money. One of his principles is that an investor should look for good investment opportunities when the market is down and exit some trades when the market is high as the market always moves in boom and bust cycles.

According to Dalio, the key to making good returns from the stock market is to invest countercyclically. He has published books which detail his investment principles, meant to guide and coach investors to adopt good investment strategies. Among the top guides are "Principles," and "A Template for Understanding Big Debt Crises," available for free as a PDF.

John Paulson

Paulson made his fortune betting against subprime mortgages at the peak of the 2007 credit bubble. While other investors recorded losses during the 2008 financial crisis, he made more than 15 billion dollars from applying a contrarian approach: betting against the market.

Based on this success, his fund attracted lots of investors, but the one event that shot him into stardom has not guaranteed continued success. As a speculative investor, he has made several wrong-footed bets on which resulted in billions of dollars in losses, such that investors began pulling their money from the fund that has shrunk from 36 billion in 2011 to under 10 billion in 2017. The fund lost 36% in 2011, lost another 14% in 2012, and this losing streak has continued with the fund consecutively recording double-digit losses from 2014-2016. As at October 2019, he has a personal net worth of 4.2 billion dollars.

Carl Celian Ichan

Investing is not all about successful streaks, even the best of them make mistakes, and Carl Celian Ichan is one such person. He is a prominent figure who made money from investing in the stock market. With a net worth over 17 billion dollars, Ichan began his career as a stockbroker, and then he started his own securities firm after he bought a seat on the New York Stock Exchange.

Buying a seat on an exchange simply means that you are now a member of the exchange and can, therefore, trade directly on an exchange. If you are not a member, then you can only trade via a broker, who is a member.

Ichan's security firm specialized in options strategies, arbitrages, and takeovers. A takeover happens when a big company wants to buy a controlling stake in another smaller company. If the smaller company refuses the offer, then the bigger company can launch a hostile bid by bidding for the company's shares directly on the stock market. Ichan made most of his money doing this and was dubbed as a "corporate raider."

Some failed attempts at takeovers left him richer due

to an increase in the share price. However, he was affected by the 2008 financial crash, where he lost 180 million. Despite the setback, he did not stop. He instead focused his business on tech companies where he acquired significant shareholdings in Netflix, Clorox, Apple, eBay, and Family Dollar (Lee, n.d.).

The Takeaway

What these cases highlight is that each investor has his own style of investing that he understands, and through the years of practicing, has been perfected in such a way that consistently makes positive returns. As an investor, you can have mentors and a team of advisers, but this is not necessarily what makes you money.

These cases also show that investments that are too risky, which most of the investors profiled here have invested in, are not for everyone. Hedging is a way of offsetting risk and this is done through short selling, credit default swaps, options, and other derivative instruments. Hedge funds, in addition to trading the usual stocks and bonds, also buy those derivative instruments and everything else in between, from fine art to racehorses, as long as there is a chance that they can make a profit.

However, there are rules. Most of the investors should be high net worth people who are called accredited investors and... That's the only rule! A hedge fund can do whatever it wants and get away with it, which should give you an idea of how risky they are. In addition to the unusual investment, they can also use leverage to maximize return, charge investors for investing in the fund, lock in funds for a certain period without paying anything to the investors—the list goes on and on.

But the bottom line is, while they can be a lucrative opportunity to make money, they are very risky. Hedge funds are only for those who have made enough capital that can cushion them against potential losses in value.
These investors did not start their investing careers in hedge funds, rather they grew their portfolios first and then moved on to hedge funds.

Chapter 8: Market Analysis

To make profits, the rule of thumb is always "buy low and sell high." But how do you know if stock is priced low? To answer this question, we need to differentiate between the "intrinsic value" of a company and its "market value."

Intrinsic value is what is known as the true value of a company which is measured through forecasting the potential earning capacity of the business as this will eventually be converted to cash flows to the shareholders in the form of dividends and capital gains. Market value, however, looks at how the market values the business as seen through the current share price on the stock exchange. These two values are not always the same.

The interaction of supply and demand forces as investors dispose of shares and others buy is what drives the market value of a company. If there are more buyers than sellers of a particular stock, the price goes up, and if there are more sellers than buyers, the price goes down. However, the action of these investors is influenced by a myriad of facts that include speculation, general industry performance, rumors, popularity of the stock amongst investors, politics, and so on. The result is that often the market value of the company may be different from its true value or intrinsic value.

In some instances, due to a surge in the demand of certain stock, the market value of some companies may be higher than the true value of the company, and such companies are said to be overvalued. Should it happen that there are overvalued shares in an investor's portfolio, these shares should be sold before value goes down such that the investor locks in or realizes capital gains. But, how can an investor know if their shares are overvalued or undervalued?

Stock market analysis is a systematic way of interrogating available data in the market to find mispriced shares. It is on the basis of this info that buy, keep, or sell decisions are made. There are two forms of market analysis, which are fundamental analysis and technical analysis.

Fundamental analysis tries to determine value through looking at fundamental/economic factors that impact the business. Questions that an investor typically answers when performing fundamental analysis are: does the company have any competitive advantage? How is the company doing financially? Does the company face a lot of competition in the industry?

Competitive advantage is a set of unique features of a company and its products that result in the company outperforming competitors. The scale of operations, capital, reputation, trade secrets, and intellectual property like patents and location governance are some examples of competitive advantages that a company may enjoy over others in the market. This positions the company to outperform competitors. Factors that are typically considered when carrying out fundamental analysis are the financial performance of the company as seen through revenues, expenses, income, growth prospects, and potential to convert all this into value for shareholders.

Using this method, an investor can practice value

investing, which is an investment strategy that involves picking stocks that are trading at a lower price relative to their fundamentals. This strategy is the best approach to making huge profits on the stock market, but it takes hard work to identify such stocks, and the profits may only be realized after a significant time lag, as the stock market may take time to correctly price the stock. As such, fundamental market analysis is typically done by investors with a long-term investment horizon.

Technical analysis is a financial analysis technique that uses market price and volume data from trading activity to determine trends and make calculated predictions about the likely movement of stock prices. This approach can be applied to any trading instrument, and in any time frame. That is, whether one is a swing trader or day trader, technical analysis is of significant use.

It is easier to conduct when compared to fundamental analysis and can also be used to identify entry and exit points, even after conducting fundamental analysis, which makes this type of market analysis important for all investors, irrespective of their trading strategy. With technical analysis, there are three main things that one needs to master before starting to trade. These are candlesticks, support and resistance levels, and patterns formed by the candlesticks. The rest of the chapter discusses each of these.

Candlesticks

These are charts that can help an investor understand what is happening to the price of a stock. Price of shares move up and down, and these charts are used to graph this price movement. The key is to always remember that these charts do not explain why the price is moving in the way it is, for that you would have to rely on fundamental analysis as was discussed above.

All known information about a stock, as in whether the company is doing well financially, is seen through its published financials, rumors of financial mismanagement, news on possible mergers and takeovers, and so on, and eventually reflected in the price. As other investors react to information, investor sentiment is also reflected in the price.

Candlestick charts use information about the price of a stock broken down into the opening price, high price, low price, and closing price for each period that is being analyzed, and this is plotted in the form of a candlestick, as shown below:

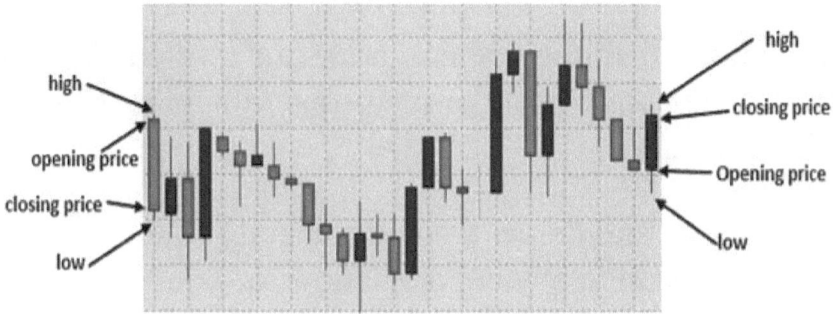

Candlestick Chart

From this picture, the candlesticks use the color blue to represent a scenario when the stock closing price was more than the opening price and the red candlesticks form when the closing price was lower than the opening price. Other colors that are normally used are a hollow body for when the closing price is higher than the opening price and a filled-in color for when the closing price is lower than the opening price.

The line above and below the colored body of the candlestick is called a wick, or shadow, or tail. So, just by glancing at a candlestick, the color of the body can tell you the period it took for the candle to form if the market closed higher or lower than the opening.

By looking at the chart, you will know if the market was bullish due to buying pressure resulting in a higher closing price or if it was bearish because there was selling pressure that was pushing the price down, and at the close, the price was lower than it was at the beginning of the period.
Once you can interpret these candlestick charts and what the colors mean, it becomes easy to interpret information and to use it to make decisions compared to looking at a bunch of numbers on a price sheet.

Setting up Your Charts

Candlestick stock charts should be set up to reflect an investors trading style. The two main types of traders, as you know, are day traders and swing traders. Day trading happens when investors open and close investment positions in a day, with no position left open overnight. For example, if you are a day trader, you may buy and sell stocks throughout the day. But your aim is to make sure that by the end of the day, you no longer have any stocks in your portfolio and have collected all your returns, be they positive or negative.

When setting up charts, the norm for day traders is to use shorter time frames such as the daily, four hour, and hourly charts. If a five-minute time frame is chosen, that means a new candle will form every five minutes, utilizing the prize information from the market to show the highest and lowest price traded and the opening and closing prices within the five minutes.

If you are looking to buy, shorter time frames, like the five-minute candles, can be used to identify the entry point that will enable you to buy at the lowest possible price. If you want to sell, you can identify the highest potential exit points to maximize profits.

Day traders use these chats to analyze short-term volatility, identify trends, and then forecast the direction that share prices are likely to move in the short-term and identify potentially profitable trades. If the charts are not set up properly, you only use four-hour charts. Each candle will only form after four hours, and a lot of volatile activity within that period that could have revealed profitable opportunities will thus be hidden.

With swing trading, investments are held over multiple days. This could be overnight, two, 50, 100 days or any other period. This allows an investor to make higher returns on their investment as stocks generally perform well over time. However, this also exposes the investor to more risks as stock prices sometimes dip if investors panic in reaction to news. Swing traders are not worried about the ups and downs that happen in the short-term and they set up their charts to focus on longer time frames such as daily, weekly, and monthly charts. These charts will thus reveal long-term trends, allowing an investor to ignore the short-term volatility. Though, short-term charts like the four hourly and the hourly can be used to identify entry and exit positions so as to maximize profits.

Indicators

Indicators are tools that use statistics from the basic candlestick data to predict changes in trends or price patterns in any traded asset and to forecast future price movement. There are two types of markets: trending markets, where the market is moving in just one direction which could be up or down, or a range-bound market where the market is moving up and down within a certain range. Indicators are split into two groups: oscillators, which identify bullish and bearish periods, and trend indicators, which only work in trending markets.

Relative strength index (RSI) is a momentum oscillator and measures the relative strength of a market against its historical price change. With this indicator, an investor can identify overbought and oversold conditions which could then be potentially sell and buy signals. An RSI value typically above 70 would indicate that the stock has been going up and is about to fall, and if acted on, an investor can lock in profits.

Moving averages are another popular indicator that show smooth lines representing average prices. If price action is consistently above the moving average trend line, then this is interpreted as a continuation of an uptrend, and if the price action moves below a trend, a reversal will be expected. Sometimes it is best to use a combination of two indicators to strengthen forecasts. An example would be using a short-term moving average indicator together with a longer-term moving average indicator. Where the two lines cross over could indicate a potential trend change.

After choosing the time frames that are compatible with your trading strategy, the next thing is to make sure that the chart is clean and easily understandable by using only a few indicators. Indicators are an important tool that can help significantly improve a trader's approach to trading, but if a chart is too cluttered with different types of indicators, you may end up getting too much conflicting information.

How to Find Good Stocks

To find good stocks, an investor needs to have a clear picture of what is really happening with the stock. That said, a combination of technical analysis and fundamental analysis can make it easy for an investor to find good stocks that are likely to result in significant gains. Good stocks for beginner investors are those that are not too risky and are preferably defensive stocks that are not significantly affected by the economy. Such stocks offer a regular dividend or record high earnings per share.

Earnings are proof that the company is currently making profits. Having identified the stocks that suit your risk profile as a beginner investor, in order to make positive returns, remember that the strategy is "buy low, sell high" all the time. Support and resistance levels are price ranges where buyers and sellers are likely to jump into action in a bid to make profits.

This action, as investors react to movement in the stock price, if properly anticipated, can help you as an investor identify good stocks to buy by correctly timing when to buy and when to sell, which will lock in significant returns.

Resistance is the price level that the stock more often

than not does not surpass. It may be gaining value, but as it approaches that level, the stock price will start to fall. Support is the lowest price that the stock is likely to drop to. To identify support and resistance, you need "confirmation," i.e. from the chart. You want to make sure that the stock did in fact reach that price level at least a few number of times before you mark that area as action signal points.

Patterns of Stock Charts

The candlesticks themselves convey information, but one other important facet of reading charts is understanding the patterns that are formed by candlesticks themselves. Patterns formed by candlesticks are important because they show the potential direction that the price of stocks can take. This potential direction is, of course, based on analyzing historical price information.

There is a belief that the market has a very long memory, and because of this, patterns that have been observed are likely to recur over and over again. Using candlesticks, it is then possible to identify these patterns and then, based on the assumptions that the pattern is recurring, try to pre-empt the market by betting that the pattern will complete as per expected.

Common patterns can be observed from these charts. Some of these patterns are called dojis, hammers, and hanging man. These patterns, when they are observed forming in charts combined with support and resistance levels, alert traders to look for opportunities to invest which may result in above-average returns.

Doji

These are candlesticks that look like a cross or a plus sign. This means that the opening and closing prices were equal, which explains why the candle has no body. These candles signal indecision in the market and could imply that trend reversal is imminent as the bears can either take control in the following period or the bulls can take control. An investor should thus start watching the market closely when they see such a pattern if they intend to enter or exit depending on how the market was trending before the doji.

Hammer

When this shape appears after a downtrend on a bullish candle, it implies a reversal. In that period, the sellers were rallying strong and pushed the price of the stock to a new low. However, toward the end of the day, last-minute buyers came through and started buying the shares at this low price, which pushed the shares up and the period closed with the highest bid.

When an investor notices a hammer forming, then they should watch the stock to see what happens next. If a hammer is followed by a bullish candle, then there is a possibility that trend reversal has been confirmed and one can look for an entry position based on this pattern.

Hanging Man

This is a bearish candle with a long wick that appears at the top after a series of up-trending candles. When this hanging man candle appears, it signals that the uptrend in probably over, and if you are holding shares, you should look for an exit position and take your profits before the price drops further.

There are other candle patterns that one can learn, but this section has demonstrated the vast amount of information that can be gleaned from just looking at candlestick charts compared to a single price sheet. Charts are thus an important tool that an investor should learn how to read before they start investing.

Chapter 9: Financial Freedom

Can you take a moment to think about all the things that you have always wanted to do, but haven't been able to because of financial constraints?
Have you set up a college fund for your children? Do you sometimes feel depressed every time you turn a year older when you realize that with each year you are getting closer and closer to retirement and you still don't know how you will pay the bills then? Do you always hold your breath whenever you drive because you know your car isn't insured? What about health care? Have you ever wanted to do a paid course that you know will advance you career-wise but couldn't because you couldn't afford it? If you lose your job tomorrow, what will happen to you? Will you worry about how you will pay off your financial debts? The list can go on.

There is a difference between living and surviving. Living is the ability to embrace life and make decisions that propel you towards self-actualization, which is the fulfilment of your potentialities. Having to hold back on doing certain things that you know are likely to improve the quality of life because you are not sure if you can handle the financial implications can result in depression and general deep-seated unhappiness. Not having the financial means to do some things, which in your opinion may be very important, is like walking around in shackles. Every time you forget your circumstance and try to run, you feel the shackles of financial inadequacy weighing you down.

If you identify with any of these scenarios, and any other that popped in your mind, then the implication is that you are not financially independent. You thus need a plan that will help you get there. A plan that will propel you from just going through life trying to dodge whatever is thrown at you to being in control of your life and living life to the fullest, on your own terms. That said, to move from where you are to a point where you achieve independence is not an event, but a process or a journey. A journey that will help you amass the wealth for you to start truly living.

This journey starts with believing that you are not just a victim of circumstances, rather you have the power to make decisions that can change your financial situation. Once you acknowledge this and are dissatisfied with the way you are currently living (or surviving) then you are ready to explore the different pathways that can liberate you financially.

The next step is learning how to manage money, which can only be done if you start budgeting. Knowing how you spend your paycheck from month to month and seeing this on a spreadsheet enables you to look at your lifestyle with a constructively critical eye. Are you spending too much money on booze and entertainment? Are you leading a healthy lifestyle? Do you have a significant portion of your paycheck that seems to just disappear, and you can't seem to account for it? Do you have a surplus every month or are you swimming in debt and you can't sustain your lifestyle without dipping into your wallet to get your credit card out month after month? Once you have come up with a budgeting system that is a true reflection of how you live in a typical month, the next step is to trim your expenses and reengineer your income to create the capacity in your budget to create wealth.

Expenses can be reduced by trimming off all unnecessary spending, like monthly subscriptions to a gym that you only go to once or twice a year, drinking sprees where you end up spending more than you expected simply because when you get drunk you end up buying rounds for everyone in the bar, etc. Check how much of your monthly cheque goes towards debt servicing, and if it's a significant chunk, then it is time to nip it in the bud by living within your means and coming up with a plan to clear all your debts, be it credit card balances, student loans, or whatever else has you in the red.

Try to clear them, and then stay clean by living within your means. A key point to note is that coming up with a plan is not going to work if the plan is not going to be implemented. Financial discipline takes commitment and a strong will to say no to certain things, which is likely to be hard. But it's worth it to go through this transition as being debt-free unlocks funds that have been going to service that debt. All that cash flow can then be used as a base to grow your wealth.

Once you are debt free, the next step is to save. Before thinking about long- term savings, you need to think about a short-term contingency fund that you can dip into should certain trigger events happen, like a loved one falling sick who must be hospitalized, car repairs, or losing your job. Again, financial discipline is the key to ensuring that you raise the required funds through monthly savings and that you ensure that the fund is only utilized for its intended purposes.

After you have achieved this, chances are high that you will already be feeling a difference in the way you view life. You can breathe easy, walk with a spring in your step, and see the silver lining. At this point, even though you are not yet there, you can now see it. Financial independence is around the corner!

Once your short-term fund is in place, you are ready to tackle your long- term financial needs. You can now think of retirement, and as your wealth accumulates, how to grow and manage your portfolio.

Long-term Trading Investment for Retirement

Investing for retirement means avoiding high risk, casino-like bets. The objective is to steadily grow the portfolio to a point where you have more than enough that you forecast as your minimum retirement needs. Short- term trading investment, which is holding assets for a short period of time and cashing in on short-term high performances is thus not a suitable approach when trading for retirement. Long-term trading ignores the short- term market fluctuations and focuses on making trades that are held for months or years, allowing the investment to steadily gain value over time.

Since the buy and hold strategy does not result in quick overnight profits, there are general rules that need to be followed when investing for retirement. The first rule is that a well-diversified portfolio works best, which shifts attention from focusing on individual stocks only to including other investment vehicles that are traded on the stock market, such as commodities, exchange-traded funds, and real estate investment trusts.

Mutual funds are also a safe bet for retirement investing, with some brokers offering robo-advisor automated online investment platforms that can offer a diversified portfolio across stocks and bonds.

The second rule is to start investing as early as possible. No one is ever too young to start thinking about retirement. Most financial institutions have retirement funds that pool money from different people who want to save for retirement and these funds are then invested in low risk, well-diversified investments with a low but steady return. At a bare minimum, you can just commit to contributing towards any one of such exchange-traded funds if you are not already doing so via a work pension fund scheme that you and your employer contribute to. With this type of retirement plan, a passive investment approach is usually acceptable.

For those who are formally employed, always participate in employer contribution pension plans, such as the 401(k) in the US. If your employer is willing to match your contributions, then this is free money that you are being offered which will bump up your accumulated fund at retirement.

There are, however, a lot of people who are either in total cost to employer contracts or who are self-employed. The onus is thus on such individuals to recognize the importance of planning for retirement and then applying financial discipline to save and invest towards retirement. Financial discipline, when combined with sound cash flow management plans, is the key to retirement planning.

Even without actively managing your investment, if you are disciplined enough to set aside money every month towards your pension, from the time you start working right up to the time you retire, you are likely to be set for retirement. If you have to do it yourself, there are investment vehicles that, when combined with stock investing, can help you strike a balance between return and risk. These vehicles are listed below:

Bonds

These are loans that you give to a government, corporation, or municipality in exchange for periodic interest payment and a return of the principal at maturity. As such, bonds will give you a steady income in the form of interest and a long-term guarantee. There are different types of bonds one can choose from based on time to maturity, riskiness, and liquidity.

Bonds are also rated, which gives you an idea of the risk that you are taking on. So, an investor can easily design a portfolio that best suits their financial needs. An investor should consider the maturity date, short-term, medium- term, and long-term, for example. Bonds are a good investment for retirement as they are unlikely to lose money, and an investor is insulated from the loss of value in the bond principal if they plan to hold the bond to maturity. The regular interest payment generates a steady stream of cash flow which can be planned for. They are also very liquid, and an investor can always liquidate his investment should the need arise.

Real estate can provide a stable source of income that also goes up in line with inflation. However, because of the sizeable capital needed to invest in real estate, most people saving towards retirement cannot afford to take this route. Real estate investment trusts (REITs), which are companies that own or manage income-producing commercial real estate, are a good alternative as retirement investment vehicles.

There are different types of REITS, such as retail, residential, health care, office, and mortgage REITs. All REITs provide high dividend yields and also provide a steady income stream. The easiest way to invest in REITs is to invest in a publicly traded REITs by purchasing shares through a broker. REITs thus enable capital-constrained investors to access real estate investment benefits, which are income, capital appreciation, diversification, and protection, just like real estate does, without the need for huge upfront capital outlays.

Annuities are a form of insurance that guarantees that, in return for a lump sum of money paid today, you will in return get a series of equal cash flows at regular intervals for a specified period of time. An annuity thus guarantees a predetermined steady income at known intervals, and this makes them attractive as an alternative investment vehicle.

It is important to recognize that investing for retirement calls for a long- term investment strategy. You cannot then lump savings intended for emergency short-term use with your retirement funds and lock them all up in the same investment vehicle where they may not be easily accessible. Savings earmarked for short-term emergency purposes should instead be invested in short-term bonds and money market instruments that are highly liquid and therefore can be converted to cash, should you need to, at no loss in value. If this rule is not adhered to, should a trigger event occur and you urgently need money, you may be forced to urgently divest some positions in the long run at a point when doing so may result in taking losses or penalties.

How to Grow Your Portfolio

Whatever an investor decides to invest in, the potential to earn a positive return from an investment should be the key decision factor if an investor is to grow their portfolio. These returns are usually in the form of interest from bonds, dividends from shares, cash flows from business, and capital gains from assets such as stocks and real estate.

With time comes experience in investing, and as experience grows, the more likely it is that you will become better at trading and identifying investments that are more suited to your investment needs. After all, experience is the best teacher. Should you make a bad investment that significantly dents your investment, don't hold on to such investments, rather limit your losses by exiting such positions.

Time allows you to lick your wounds, learn from your mistakes, and forge ahead and recover from bad investments. Bad investment decisions are unlikely to be made if an investor always invests in what they understand. There is a lot of information that is available to investors. But if you do not understand what you invested in in detail, how can you sift through all this information and isolate that which is likely to have an impact on your investment? if you can't sift, then you may have information that you can act on that can earn you significant returns or which, if acted on, can help you avoid losses.

Financial Freedom via Stock Market Investment

Once you have your rainy-day fund set up, and your retirement needs catered for, you can then focus on achieving financial freedom. The stock market is one such fertile place and, as was shown in Chapter 5, evidence abounds of investors who have made it big through stock market investments.

In order to achieve the best returns from investing in the stock market, the key is to focus on just a few stocks. This is a strategy that differs from what you would do when making investments for retirement, because the main focus there is low risk, steady but low returns from a well-diversified portfolio that guarantees that you will have enough funds after retirement.

As necessary as it is to have a retirement plan, it is not enough if you want financial freedom. Once you have chosen your few growth stocks, monitor them, get to understand the company and the industry, develop the skill to decipher news and fish out what is likely to drive prices in your invested stocks, and be ready to strike and lock in gains.

As a beginner investor, it is best to limit your portfolio to just two stocks. That way you can do effective industry analysis to identify your entry points and you get to concentrate your money in stocks that are likely to be winners. It is important to know that successful investing that is going to create significant wealth is not based on luck but is a well-thought-out process that is fortified by good planning, a commitment to set the plan in motion, and discipline.

To get financial freedom, you need to set realistic long-term goals, which means defining your investment horizon and your target return and having the capital you need to get there. And then take the plunge. The thought of risking hard-earned capital may be daunting at first, but as you immerse yourself in trading, learning as you go, and making deliberate informed decisions, you may realize that the stock market is not as risky as you thought. That might pull you out of your shell and change your risk perceptions and what you are willing to risk to gain financial freedom.

With experience, also comes maturity. This maturity is seen in the ability to control one's emotions in the process of monitoring investments. The ability to make logical decisions is what will enable you, as an investor, to look past the short-term volatility that abounds and focus on the long-term. This is what differentiates successful traders from the rest in a market where a lot of people trade based on rumors, speculation, fear, and hope, instead of logic derived from a thorough analysis of a company's assets, prospects, and management (Lewis, n.d.).

Conclusion

What this book has shown throughout is that wealth from investing is not something that happens overnight. Applying yourself, consistently trading, and learning from your mistakes should you make negative returns (and this happens to the best of them, and they never gave up!), satisfying your thirst of knowledge through researching should you face a situation you do not understand and are not sure of how to proceed is the way to go. This practical experience is the knowledge that is interna0lized and is what will eventually make you money.

All the successful investor listed in Chapter 7 did not make their fortune overnight. What they have today reflects decades of investing in the stock market, constantly scanning the market for opportunities, and taking action by committing their capital in order to get investment returns. Without capital, it is impossible to start building wealth, and being debt free is the first step towards being wealthy.

Since investing is all about putting capital at risk in return for reward, it can only work if that capital is equity capital—your own money, not debt. This point cannot be overemphasized, as with all trades that happen there is a chance that an investor may suffer losses. Keep in mind that no investment strategy is completely foolproof, and as a result, investing in the stock exchange with borrowed funds will only sink you deeper into poverty if your investments do not pay off.

An alternative approach to maximizing the capital that you can employ when investing is to get other people to invest in your ideas. But you cannot do that successfully if you have not yet developed a demonstrable winning strategy yourself that you can then use to convince other people to buy in on. For this to happen, you guessed it right, you need your own capital!

Once a good capital base has been built, it should then be possible to invest in riskier investments—but for now, keep it simple!